Preface:

We live in the world of uncertainty and unknown but greatly influenced by them, largely from progress in technology, in social, cultural, political and in financial.

Bit coins with an idea of block chain, Wikipedia and A.I. (artificial intelligence) are some of the prominent phenomenon. The World of Japanese Garden could not stay outside of these phenomena.

While I still do not understand them fully, I have decided to jump in this unknown world to study the impact of these on our current work on Japanese Garden and participate in exploring to develop definition of Japanese Garden.

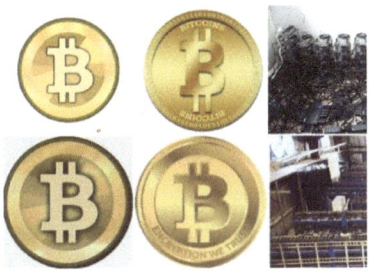

(Photo 02)

If we do not participate and anticipate, we will be overshadowed and overpowered by other participants from Wikipedia and A.I and others who may not concern themselves on Japanese Garden. and which has been taking place already.

Ahead of all the studies and surveys conducted in this book, I am listing here three versions of definition of Japanese Garden to promote further discussion, to appeal to the public and eventually make this appear in Wikipedia.

Version One:

Japanese garden is a space where there is a sense of connection to the cosmos, universe and eternity.

Version Two:

A space where there is a sense of connection to the cosmos, universe and eternity.
Japanese garden is a space where there is a sense of connection to the cosmos, universe and eternity.

The Japanese garden is
A space where there is a sense of recalling natural landscape and changing of time.
A space where there is a linkage to Japanese culture and history.
A space where there is a sense of connectedness to the cosmos, universe and eternity.

Version Three:

Japanese garden is a space where there is a sense of connection to the cosmos, universe and eternity.

The Japanese garden is
A space where there is a sense of recalling natural landscape and changing of time.
A space where there is a linkage to Japanese culture and history.
A space where there is a sense of connectedness to the cosmos, universe and eternity.

A combination of stationary and sequential organization,
with symmetrical, natural and non axial layout, and employing traditional design method and technique and mostly natural materials.

私はここで、この本で行われた調査の詳述に先立って、さらなる議論を促し、一般の人々にアピールし、最終的にWikipediaにけいさいさせる為に　私の　暫定的結論としての日本庭園の定義の3つのバージョンを列記します。

バージョン1：

日本の庭は、宇宙,そして永遠につながる感覚がある空間です。

バージョン2：

日本の庭は、宇宙,そして永遠につながる感覚がある空間。

"Japanese Garden Defined:
In the World of Bit Coin, Wikipedia and A.I. But Why?"

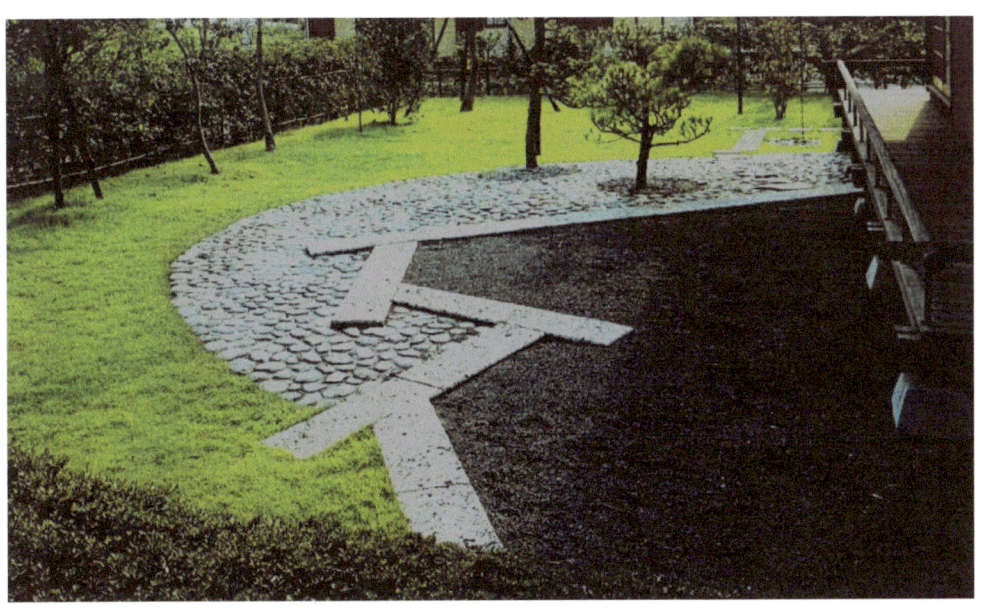

Koichi Kobayashi

Contents:

Chapter 1: Introduction
Chapter 2: Proposal
Chapter 3: Overview of Background
Chapter 4: Preceding Studies, Seminars and Workshops
Chapter 5: Significance and Need of Definition
Chapter 6 : Preceding Definition and Evaluation
Chapter 7: Image of the Japanese Garden
Chapter 8: Is there boundary for Japanese Garden?
Chapter 9: Overviews of Japanese Garden for the Future
Chapter 10: Qualification in Definition
Chapter 11: Definition Proposed

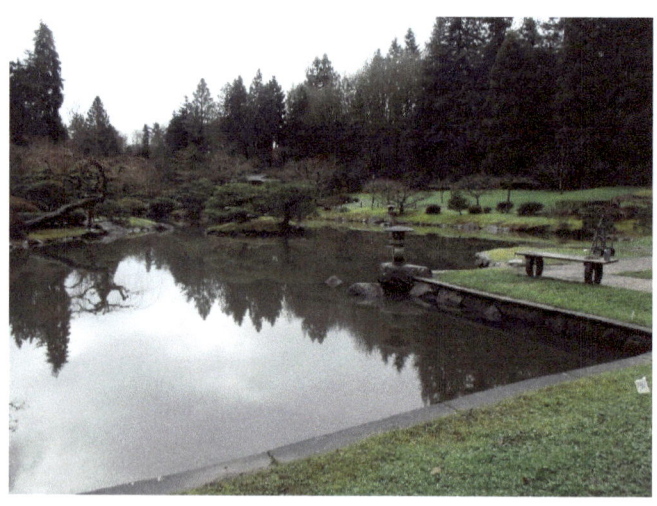

(Photo 01)

日本の庭は
自然景観を思い起こさせ、時間を変える感覚がある空間。

日本の文化と歴史とのつながりがある空間。

自然景観を思い起こさせ、時間を変える感覚がある空間。

バージョン3：

日本の庭は、宇宙、そして永遠につながる感覚がある空間です。

日本の庭は、
自然景観を思い起こさせ、時間を体感する感覚がある空間。

日本の文化と歴史とのつながりがある空間。

その　構成においては固定的とシークエンスの組み合わせ、
対称的また、自然かつ非対称的なレイアウトと、
伝統的なデザイン手法と技術を　もちいて意匠され、材料はほとんどが天然素材である。

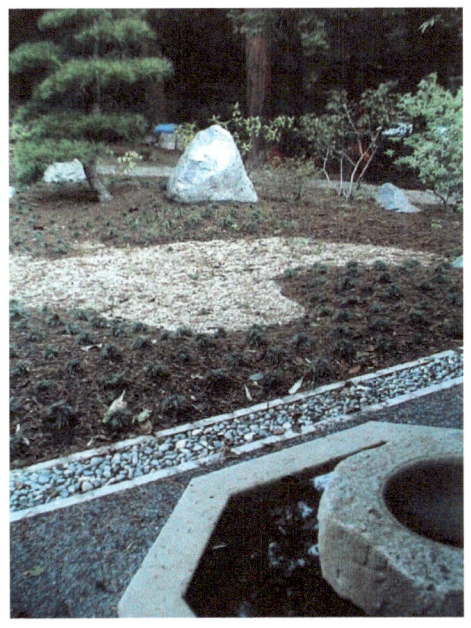

(Photo 03)

Chapter 1: Introduction

At the time of the Fourth International Conference of Japanese Garden in Seattle in 2001, Professor Takeo Uesugi of California Polytechnique University, Pomona stated the following regarding the future of Japanese Garden.

> *In the past centuries, we have experienced a marvelous propagation of Japanese Gardens outside of Japan as a result of the tremendous contributions of many talented professionals to the field of design, construction and maintenance of Japanese Gardens. Furthermore, the strong presence and influence of today's Japanese Gardens has permeated many aspects of our contemporary society, including landscape industry, spirituality, art, and culture. With its strong aesthetic appeal and timely themes of spirituality and nature, Japanese Gardens have established itself as respected force in modern landscape architecture in Japan and in overseas countries. As we continue into the new Millennium, we usher into an exciting new era of evolutionary change in the appreciation, understanding, design and functionality of Japanese Gardens. We now come to understand that while Japanese Gardens have been shaped by a rich history grounded in Japanese culture, it is, at the same time, not bound by these time honored traditions. The future of Japanese Gardens must transcend our current understanding of this traditional art form as we seek to expand our perspectives of what a Japanese Garden is, and can be.*

Originally I started writing an initial paper to create an introduction as to how best to develop, design and foster Japanese Garden abroad, primarily in the North America. But this task is a vain without clearly understanding what the Japanese Garden is.

Japanese garden has been said to be an important aspects of Japanese culture which nurtures international understanding and friendship. Many Japanese gardens have been built as products of attraction to things oriental, government public relations in form of expositions, friendship-sister city relationship, showing of wealth of individuals and others over the years in America and in Europe.

Even though these initial roles still exist, today the role of public and private Japanese gardens, especially in the North America has expanded beyond landscaping and recreation; they are used in commercial settings, for weddings and events, for cultural programs for professional medical therapy and more.

There are over 500 Japanese Gardens existing today throughout the world mainly in North America and in Europe. Some of these date well back over a hundred years in history. There are many gardens facing extinction and major changes as it has been taking place in Japan as well. There are due to historical, social and mainly fiscal reasons. But there are a good many Japanese Gardens abroad thriving even today's uncertain time.

A number of new gardens have been created and still in progress. I hold that some of them are not resonating with me for one reason or another. I am, however, observing recurrent problems gardens facing changes in a name of making the gardens adapting to modern requirements and sustainability which could be contrary o the soul of Japanese garden and problems in creation of gardens which astray from the essence of Japanese garden in my understanding.

Many questions have to be answered in countering these problems. These may include:

What is Japanese garden (in Japan) ?, and What is Japanese garden abroad?

How has Japanese Garden been viewed and appreciated by people abroad?

Can you define "What is Japanese Garden?" for creating a new Japanese garden in a simple and clear manner for gardens outside of Japan? Or is that possible, productive and meaningful? Without heavy reliance on understanding of symbolism?

What is an emerging value for Japanese garden in Japan and abroad?

What could be the design process most suited for gardens outside of Japan?

What is the future of Japanese Garden abroad?

I am attempting to write about a complex world of Japanese garden as simple and clear manner as possible and as graphically as possible.

Now you can find definition in Wikipedia on almost anything including garden as it is linked with such search engine as Google, Yahoo and others.. They may be of quality or worse. And most of us do not know how these are produced and monitored if at all. But this is to stay just as Bitcoins may do.

Following table shows Definition found in the Wikipedia and Encyclopedia Britanica On Line today. Do you concur with any if not all in Wikipedia and Online on gardens ?

(Table 01)

Garden and Country	Source		Source
	Wikipedia.com		Ency.Britan/Dictionary Encyclopedia.com EncyclopediaBritanica.com
Japanese Garden	Japanese gardens (*nihon teien*) are traditional gardens[1] whose designs are accompanied by Japanese aestheticand philosophical ideas , avoid artificial ornamentation, and highlight the natural landscape. Plants and worn, aged materials are generally used by Japanese garden designers to suggest an ancient and faraway natural		Japanese garden, in landscape design, a type of garden whose major design aesthetic is a simple, minimalist natural setting designed to inspire reflection and meditation.

	landscape, and to express the fragility of existence as well as time's unstoppable advance.[2] Ancient Japanese art inspired past garden designers.[2] By the Edo period, the Japanese garden had its own distinct appearance.	
French Garden	The French formal garden, also called the *jardin à la française* (literally, "garden in the French manner" in French), is a style of garden based on symmetry and the principle of imposing order on nature. Its epitome is generally considered to be the Gardens of Versailles designed during the 17th century by the landscape architect André Le Nôtre for Louis XIV and widely copied by other European courts……	Not included
Italian Garden	The Giardino all'italiana (Italian pronunciation: [dʒarˈdiːno alˌlitaˈljaːna]) or Italian garden is stylistically based on symmetry, axial geometry and on the principle of imposing order over nature. It influenced the history of gardening, especially French gardens and English gardens……	Not included
English Garden	The English landscape garden, also called English landscape park or simply the English garden (French: *Jardin à l'anglaise*, Italian: *Giardino all'inglese*, German: *Englischer Landschaftsgarten*, Portuguese: *Jardim inglês*, Spanish: *Jardín inglés*), is a style of "landscape" garden which emerged in England in the early 18th century, and spread across Europe, replacing the more formal, symmetrical *jardin à la*	English garden, French Jardin Anglais, type of garden that developed in 18th-century England, originating as a revolt against the architectural garden, which relied on rectilinear patterns, sculpture, and the unnatural shaping of trees.

	française of the 17th century as the principal gardening style of Europe.[1] The English garden presented an idealized view of nature. It drew inspiration from paintings of landscapes by Claude Lorrain and Nicolas Poussin, and, in the Anglo-Chinese garden, from the classic Chinese gardens of the East,[2] …..	The revolutionary character of the English garden lay in the fact that, whereas gardens had formerly asserted man's control over nature, in the new style, man's work was regarded as most successful when it was indistinguishable from nature's. In the architectural garden the eye had been directed along artificial, linear vistas that implied man's continued control of the surrounding countryside, but in the English garden a more natural, irregular formality was achieved in landscapes consisting of expanses of grass, clumps of trees, and irregularly shaped bodies of water.
Chinese Garden	The Chinese garden is a landscape garden style which has evolved over three thousand years. It includes both the vast gardens of the Chinese emperors and members of the imperial family, built for pleasure and to impress, and the more intimate gardens created by scholars, poets, former government officials, soldiers and merchants, made for reflection and escape from the outside world. They create an idealized miniature landscape, which is meant to express the harmony that should exist between man and nature……	Not included
Islamic Garden	Traditionally, an Islamic garden is a cool place of rest and reflection, and a reminder of paradise. The Qur'an has many references to gardens, and the garden is used as an earthly analogue for the life in paradise which is promised to believers: The general theme of a traditional	

	Islamic garden is water and shade, not surprisingly since Islam came from and generally spread in a hot and arid climate. Unlike English gardens, which are often designed for walking, Islamic gardens are intended for rest and contemplation. For this reason, Islamic gardens usually include places for sitting......		
Korean Garden	Korean gardens are natural, informal, simple and unforced, seeking to merge with the natural world.[1] Korean gardens were developed under the influences of the Chinese gardens. They have a history that goes back more than two thousand years,[2] but are little known in the west. The oldest records date to the Three Kingdoms period (57 BC- 668 AD)		

Following table illustrates some of the key words used in these definition and number of word count as a reference.

(Table 02)

Garden and Country	Source	Key Words	Number of letters
	Wikipedia.com		
Japanese Garden:	traditional gardens[1] whose designs are accompanied by Japanese aestheticand philosophical ideas, avoid artificial ornamentation, and highlight the natural landscape Ancient Japanese art inspired past garden designers.[2] By the Edo period, the Japanese garden had its own distinct appearance.[3]	Japanese Aesthetic Philosophy Natural Landscape Japanese Art	554
French Garden:	garden based on symmetry and the principle of imposing order on nature.	Symmetry Order on nature	407

Italian Garden:	based on symmetry, axial geometry and on the principle of imposing order over nature.	Symmetry Order on nature	249
English Garden	an idealized view of nature. It drew inspiration from paintings of landscapes been described by European travellers.[2] The English garden usually included a lake, sweeps of gently rolling lawns set against groves of trees, ○ ○ ○ ○ ○	Idealized nature Landscape painting Characteristic Garden Features	1268
Chinese Garden:	It includes both the vast gardens of the Chinese emperors and members of the imperial family, built for pleasure and to impress, and the more intimate gardens created by scholars, poets, former government officials, soldiers and merchants, made for reflection and escape from the outside world. an idealized miniature landscape,○ ○ ○ ○ ○ •	Idealized miniature landscape Characteristic Garden Features	740
Islamic Garden:		Rest and reflection Paradise Characteristic Garden Features	233
Korean Garden:		Natural, informal and unforced	151

Chapter 2: Proposal

I will attempt to illustrate the following in this presentation (paper).

1. Provide overviews of background on Japanese Garden and
2. Identify need and significance in defining Japanese Garden and
3. Develop quality (attributes) for the definition and
4. Propose definition ranging from simple to complex and

5. Prepare this proposal as graphically as possible for the ease of understanding.

Identification of the needs and significance has been conducted over the last few years through literature research and surveys and interviews with more than one hundred individuals with a diverse back grounds and nationalities, at times of lectures, seminars and conferences I conducted or attended in Japan and abroad.

Chapter 3: Overview of Background

Before diving further into the discussion of definition, following shows my understanding of Japanese Garden in history and diversity of design: its style and spatial composition so that I and readers all can share common understanding on Japanese Garden. It is intended to illustrate evolutionary process of Japanese Garden throughout the history which still has been taking place.

History and Evolution of the Japanese Garden

(Table 03)

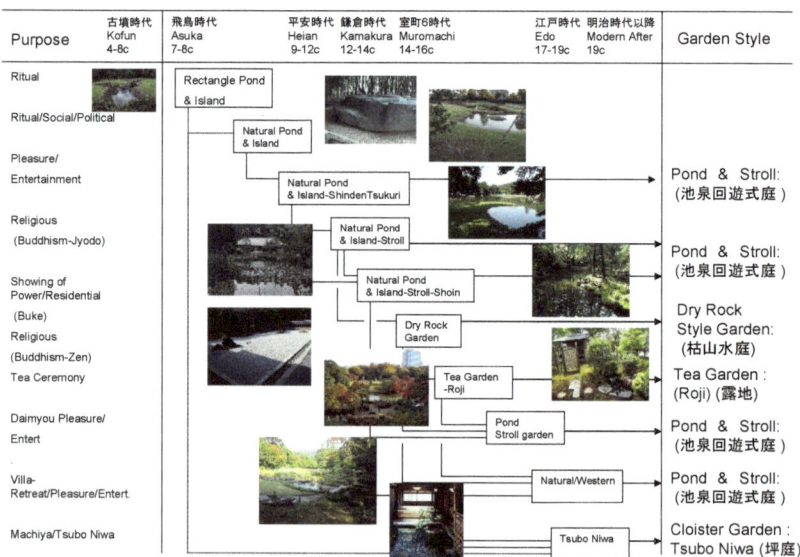

Following table illustrates development of Japanese Garden and its major contributors including Tachibana Toshitsuna (Saku Tei Ki), Muso Soseki (Moss Temple), Senno Rikyu (Tea ceremony), Kobori Enshuu (Katsura Villa), and Uyeji (Murina Ann). I could add Shigemori MIrei, Iida Juki, Kenzo Ogata and Yoshikuni Araki to name a few.

(Table 3A)

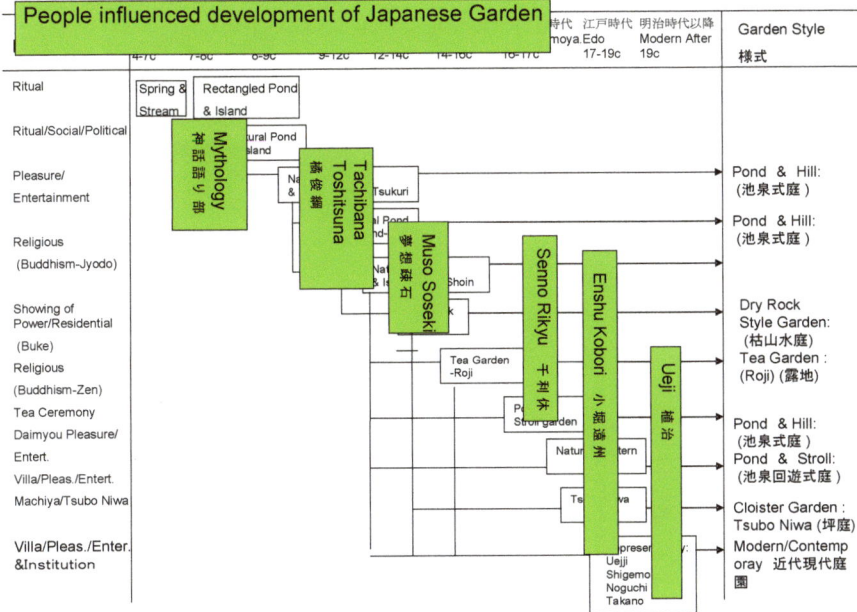

Following figures illustrate comparison of diverse garden styles of the world in a simple graphic.

(Figure 01)

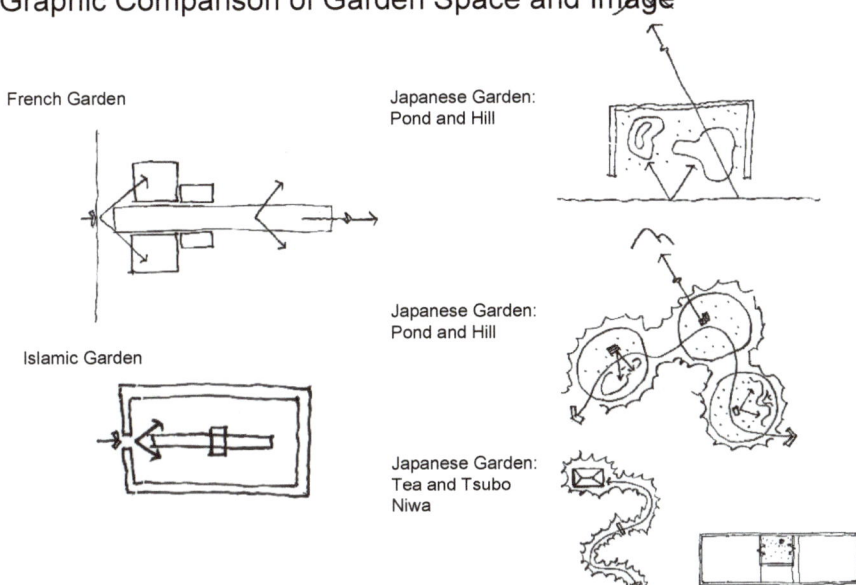

(Figure 02)

Graphic Comparison of Garden Space and Image

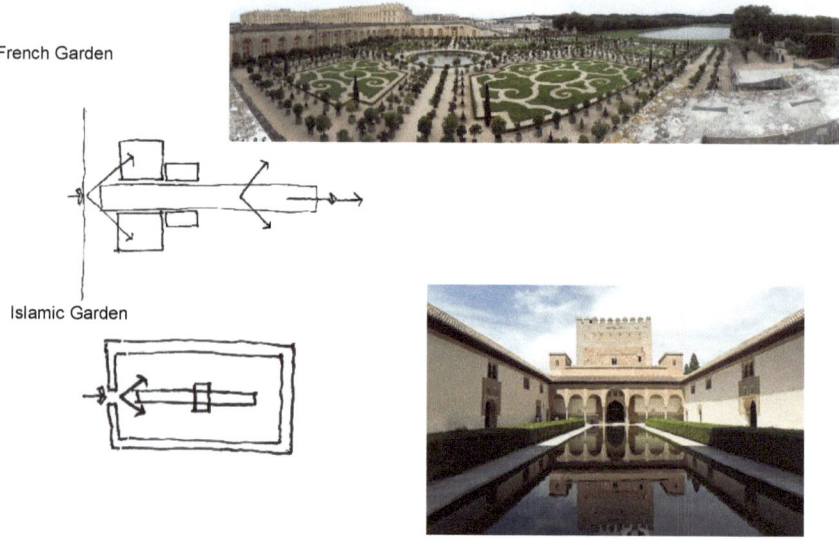

French Garden

Islamic Garden

(Figure 03)

Graphic Comparison of Garden Space and Image

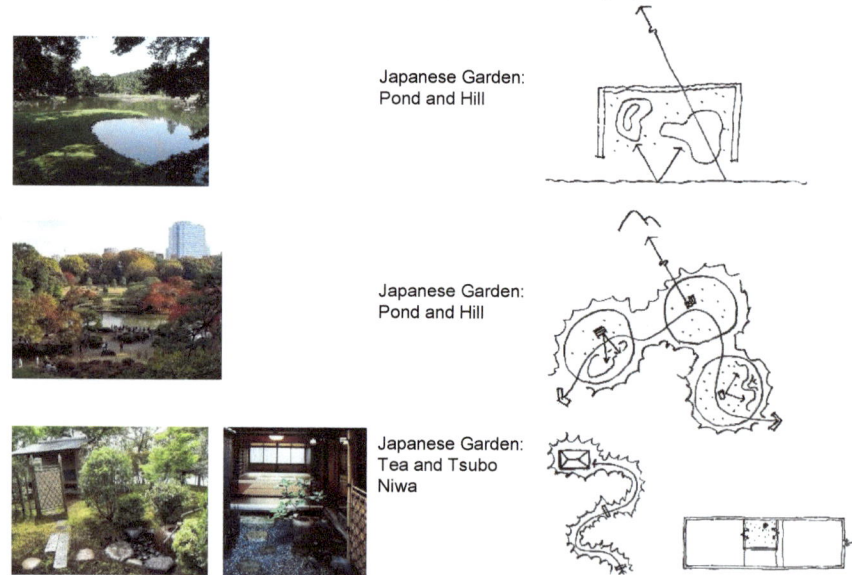

Japanese Garden:
Pond and Hill

Japanese Garden:
Pond and Hill

Japanese Garden:
Tea and Tsubo Niwa

(Figure04)

Graphic Comparison of Garden Space and Image

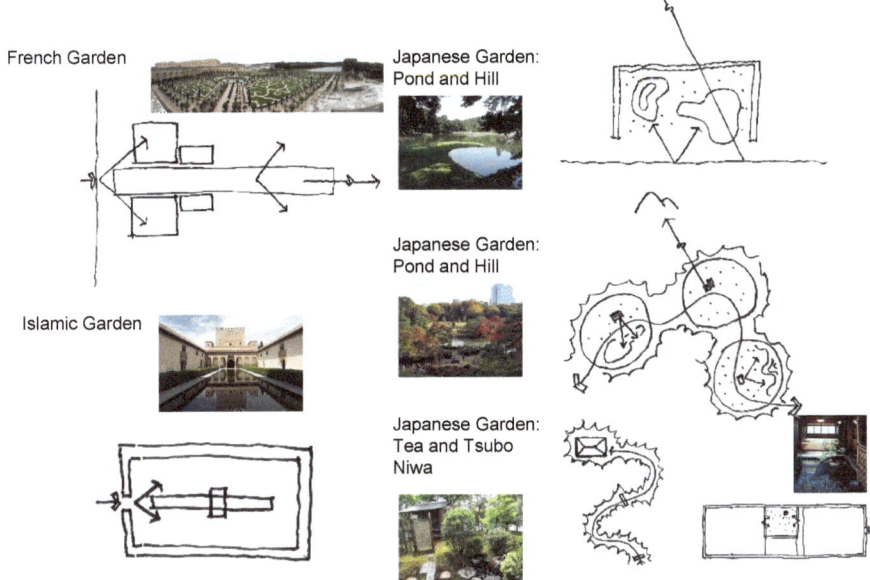

Following tables illustrate a system of classification of the Japanese Garden and simplified comparison of the gardens in the world.

A system of classification of the Japanese Garden

(Table 04)

Traditional Japanese garden	Traditional composition: Land use and purpose 　　Pond-Hill 　　Rock Garden 　　Path and Tea 　　Tsuboniwa (Cloister)　etc. Traditional technique　including dynamic symmetry, natural form, sequencing, borrowed scenery, enflaming and others Natural material Imageability, Spirituality, Abstraction and Symbolism
Evolving Japanese Garden or Japanese Influenced Garden	Chiefly traditional composition: Unlimited land use and purpose Chiefly traditional technique Unlimited use of material Not limited to Imageability, Spirituality, Abstraction and Symbolism

Simplified comparison of gardens in the world

(Table 05)

Country/Style	Symbolism, Religion and Spirituality
Japanese	Buddhism, Shinto and Tea
English	Not apparent
French	Authoritarian
Italian	Authoritarian
Islamic	Moslem
Chinese	Buddhism, Taoism, Confucian

(Table 06)

Country/Style	Layout & Form	Topography	Use of water	Use of Plant
Japanese	Natural/Informal	Varied	Natural basin and flow	Mostly natural
English	Natural/Informal	Varied	Natural Basin	Natural
French	Axial and symmetry	Flat／sloping	Pond and fountain	Horticultural
Italian	Axial and symmetry	Terraced	Fountain and cascade	Horticultural
Islamic	Formal	Flat	Canal and spray	Ornamental
Chinese	Natural/Informal	Varied	Natural basin and flow	Mostly natural

Chapter 4: Preceding Studies, Seminars and Workshops

Preceding studies, seminars and workshops if not conferences have been held on the subject of defining Japanese garden. A representative of these are listed in a summary format below.

Title of this seminar, organized by the Garden Society of Japan was " Enjoy Today's Garden" in 2014, discussion held centered on essence of (Japanese Garden) with a strong implication to defining Japanese Garden.

Conclusion of the seminar stated that when asked "What is a good garden? Then the answer is "It is a garden resonating with your heart".

(Figure 05 &6) Reprinted from Niwa Magazine

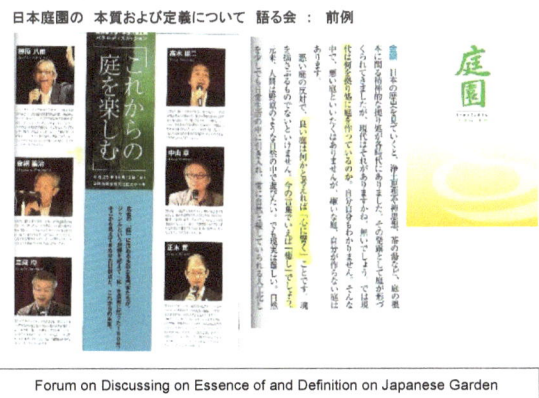

Forum on Discussing on Essence of and Definition on Japanese Garden

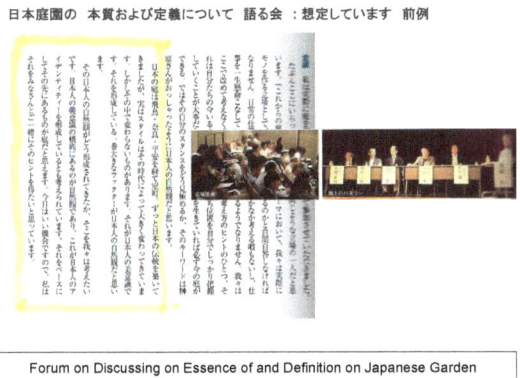

Forum on Discussing on Essence of and Definition on Japanese Garden

It further stated that even though there is a diverse styles of Japanese Garden, in there we can find thing that has not changed over time. It is " the attitude of Japanese toward nature or naturalness".
(Table 07)

Hahiro Sakakibara	Natural forces such as providence and regularity. I must explain it concretely and theoretically. . . Beauty is not going to be theoretically crawling under the root of where it is born. . .
Kenji Takamizu	I think that the real goodness of Japan is in the beauty that coexists with nature and is old. . .
Shigeji Kanatsuna	It is not Japanese, French, or Western, but something that echoes something human beings, that is shaken by the soul. . . A good garden is "to respond to your heart" if you think something. . . It will heal. . .

Akira Nakamura	Ryotaro Shiba at the Japan Architects Association says that "Japanese garden is the best in the world"...
Hachiro Sakakibara	Natural forces such as providence and regularity. I must explain it concretely and theoretically... Beauty is not going to be theoretically crawling under the root of where it is born...
Noriko Kawai	In order to raise the recognition of the Japanese garden, in order to cultivate the world market and to be accepted globally (like UNESCO World Heritage Sites) we need high definition ...
Jeff Burton	Clear definition of Japanese garden was required in designation for US national park :Japane American Internment Historic Site
Garden Society of Japan: Committee for UNESCO World Heritage Designation	Preparing for listing with UNESCO World Heritatge
Ministry of Land and Construction: Committee on Japanese Garden Abroad	For providing support to Japanese gardens in Japan and abroad in order to increase awareness and leading new market and tourism.

A number of conferences, seminars and workshops had been held to discuss definition of Japanese garden in Japan and abroad at such places as Kyoto, Tokyo, Vancouver and Seattle.

Participants at events:

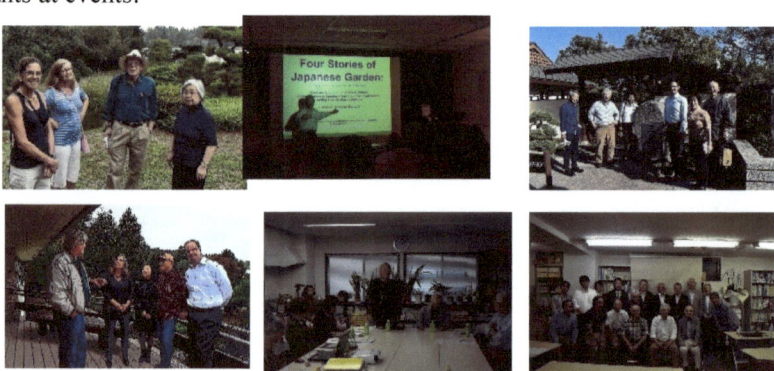

(Photo 04)

A group panel presentation after a year long communication among panelists will be held at time of the World Japanese Garden Conference: the North American Japanese Garden Association in Portland, 2018.

I organized this panel with the following out line:

Time has come to a point when we start preparing structure for our panel presentation and discussion.

Following is my idea to be further developed with you.
We have 150 minutes altogether among us.

Having a simultaneous interpretation at the conference is not definite.

Here is my idea: divide 150 minutes to three parts as follows:
- Part A. Introduction and Common Questions
- Part B. Topics as related to panel theme
- Part C. Questions and Answers

We could allocate time as follows:
* Scenario 1: Part A, 5 minutes for each, total of 30 minutes
              Part B, 15 minutes for each, total of 90 minutes
              Part C, total of 30 minutes

* Scenario 2: Part A, 3 minutes for each, total of 30 minutes
              Part B, 18 minutes for each, total of 108 minutes
              Part C, total of 12 minutes

Description of Parts:

* Part A. Introduction and Common Questions

State responses to:
1. the Need and Significance of working with definition and to
2. the stated reasons for and against to this work
3. and state counter responses
4. and to state your preliminary definition

* Part B. Topics as related to panel theme, as stated in your proposal

  Noriko Kawai :
  A monograph on the possible growth of real estate market and Japanese gardens in the world market

  Koichi Kobayashi :
  How is our work on defining Japanese garden been proceeding?

  Edzard Teubert:
  Smart Garden; Smarter landscape: Smart Cities

  Fumiaki Takano:
  Beyond Albert Kahn Japanese Garden: Design and Construction in Paris, France

Seiko Goto presents :
The spatial effects of Japanese Garden-Symbolism and Design

Carla Amorim :
Vision of definition of Japanese garden in Europe

- Part C. Questions and Answers with audience to be moderated by Kobayashi

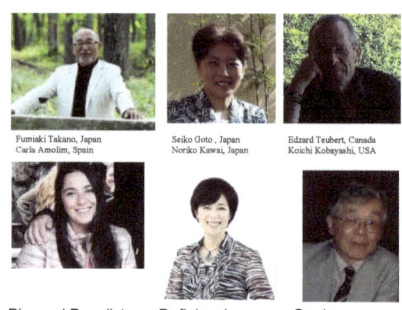

Planned Panelists on Defining Japanese Garden :
NAJGA 2018, Portland

(Photo 05)

Survey is conducted to identify words and sentences which resonate most closely with the essence and definition of Japanese Garden found in web pages from representative Japanese gardens in the North America and association. The following illustrates a summary from this survey:

Elizabeth Hubert Malott Japanese Garden at Chicago Botanical Garden

reflecting the yin-yang balance between the ephemeral existence of human life and the timelessness of nature….illusion of age. …a representation of nature…to purify themselves, both physically (by washing their hands and drinking the water) and spiritually (by symbolically washing away their cares)…reflect the fleeting quality of human life

Montreal Botanical Garden: Japanese Garden
peace and harmony, away from the rapid pace of modern life life and renewal. the expression of nature and symbolizes renewal, calm, wonder and continuity in the hereafter. Stones, symbol of duration and of the omnipresence of the forces of the nature, the light of knowledge clearing away the clouds of ignorance…..their interest for the plant realm ….the universal forms of life…cultural and social activities at the Japanese Garden

Morikami Garden
(None discovered)

Nitobe Memorial Garden
goal was "to become a bridge across the Pacific." ….an idealized conception and symbolic representation of nature….,the garden is designed to suggest a

span of time ……. "devil-losing bridge….a symbol of longevity…. Nitobe lantern is rich with symbols

San Diego Japanese Friendship Garden
seeks to foster a relationship between humans and nature, providing a respite attuned to Japanese simplicity, serenity, and aestheticism.

Portland Japanese Garden
Inspiration, serenity, tranquility, and the aestheticism of nature…..The expression of Japanese culture, tradition, and aesthetics.

Yume Japanese Garden of Tucson
expression of an ancient Japanese heritage   the creative force of centuries of Japanese culture

Seattle Japanese Garden
shizensa, the essence of nature

North American Japanese Garden Association
A kinder, healthier and more beautiful world through Japanese gardens.

A few of these gardens include any reference on what their garden is about and maintaining and fostering to be.

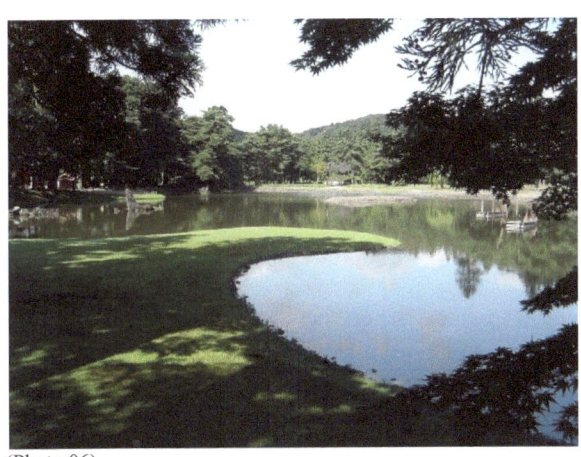
(Photo 06)

Chapter 5: Significance and Need of Definition

1. Attitude toward defining Japanese Garden

A series of survey have been conducted from diverse group of professionals and non professionals to identify their attitude toward working on defining Japanese Garden Summary of this survey is graphically shown in a diagram below.

(Table 08)

Responses on the need/significance on definition

Group Z : Con/Against/Neutral
Offshore designers with Japanese experience

Respndent	Description
Marc Kean, USA	My honest answer is that I do not think it is necessary to attempt to define what a Japanese garden is. Not from my point of view as a designer in any case. I also do not think it is possible to truly define what a Japanese garden is.
David Sloason, USA	To be honest, I don't see a need for exploring the definition of Japanese Gardens. What good would it do? Seeking such a definition does not engage the student in experiential learning and therefore is a waste of time.
Christian Tagsold, Germany	I think definitely yes but only to find out what people think, not to develop a better or even perfect definition which in my opinion is futile.
Ken Brown, USA	I agree with Christian that a single definition of Japanese garden is not very helpful. Perhaps Christian ad I are raised in the academic environment that says that almost all meanings are contingent, open to change based on context and over time.

Survey with the following questions had been distributed:
1. Is there needs for exploring definition on Japanese Garden?
2. What is definition?
3. What definition exist today? Historical precedents? Any concerns?
4. How are they compared to definitions for gardens in other culture and countries?
5. How definition could be developed to be productive in designing and management of Japanese garden?
6. Develop and agree on Definition

Responses from surveys are plotted according to the following indication:
- On horizontal axis: whether responses are showing leaning toward subjective (thus leading to more flexibility in definition), or leaning toward objective (thus leaning to more rigidity in definition).
- On vertical axis: whether responses are pursuing for higher degree of appreciation toward establishing comparison and significance or pursuing for higher degree of innovativeness and sensibility.

Attitude of leading designers and researchers are plotted on base diagram and shown below as an example.

(Figure 07)

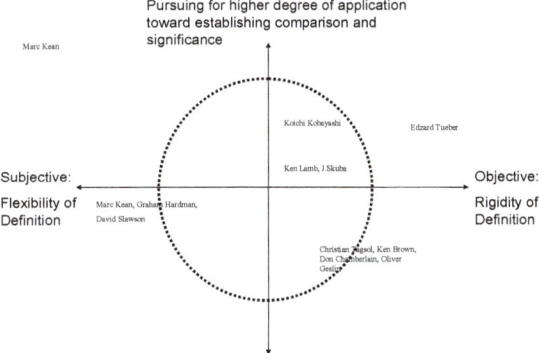

(Figure 08)

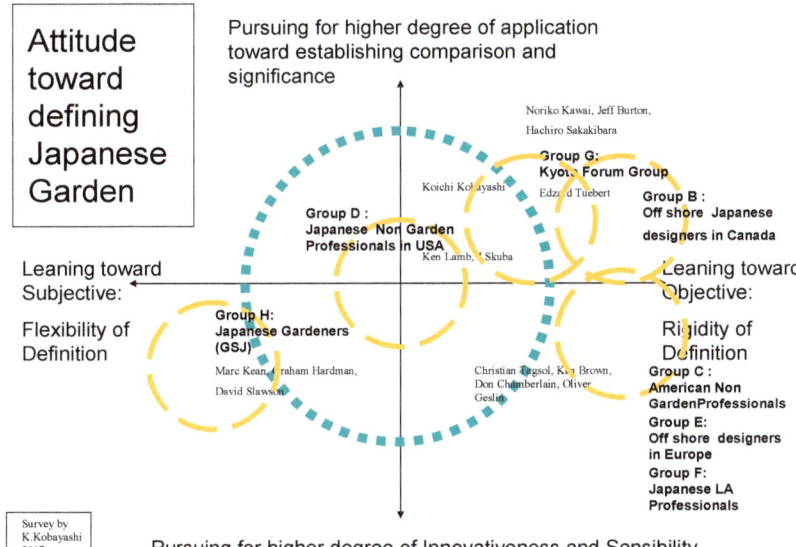

A complete listings of attitude survey from participants is included in Appendix.

Two strong conclusions are drawn from this plotting and overlaying indicate that

(1). Japanese garden designers abroad and Off shore Japanese Garden designers (Japanese) are found on the opposite side of horizontal axis (subjective vs. objective).

(2). No strong indication is found on vertical axis.

(3). Opinion leaders (mainly from Group H) tend to lean toward subjective ness as compared to other leaders from Groups of B,G and F, Individual responses on "Attitude toward defining Japanese Garden" is included in Appendix.

2. Disagreement

Through these surveys, following reasons are identified as to why defining Japanese Garden is not significant and not needed by some leading experts.

1. It is so diverse, elusive and complex
2. It constrains free and innovative thinking
3. It resides in ones brain and it can be gotten when see garden
4. it is in one's intuitiveness and not logical
5. It can only be understood on site not at desk
6. It cannot be written down

How can we address to each of these?

Following table is an attempt to illustrate degree of complexity and constraints in defining Japanese Garden as I have identified.

(Table 09)

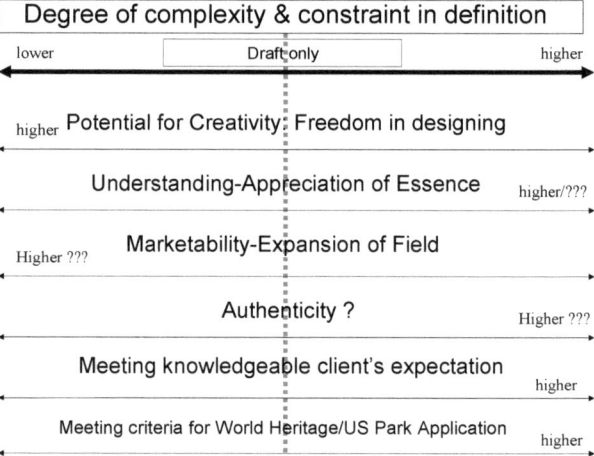

3. Statement of Need and Significance in Developing Commonly Agreed, workable and Defendable Definition

The foundation for maintaining the Japanese garden is to have experts who understand the importance, characteristics, technology and materials of Japanese gardens. The current and future trends in supply of these experts in North America are indicated by the annihilation of the Japanese Garden Association in Seattle and California in the twentieth century. However, at the same time, as seen in the planning of new gardens such as Portland, Fargo, Vancouver and Washington DC, the demand for creation and training of high quality Japanese gardens is expanding. Many of these are for public institutions and private recruiters who have received highly valued education. In promoting design and construction, it is necessary to define Japanese gardens practically and with high quality there is. Academic examples in defining Japanese gardens to be applied to the North America have limitations. Most of them are in Japanese sentences, not English. Under today's social change seeking a more systematic and logical approach and the informationization era of globalization, we need to correct this situation not only in Japan but also in the North America.

Most existing studies that define Japanese gardens in English in the English language are in descriptive qualitative form and do not conform to the definition of the word "definition" and may not be based on scientific research methods. It is necessary to create definitions that require extensive research, such as questionnaire surveys and interviews with features and images of the Japanese garden.

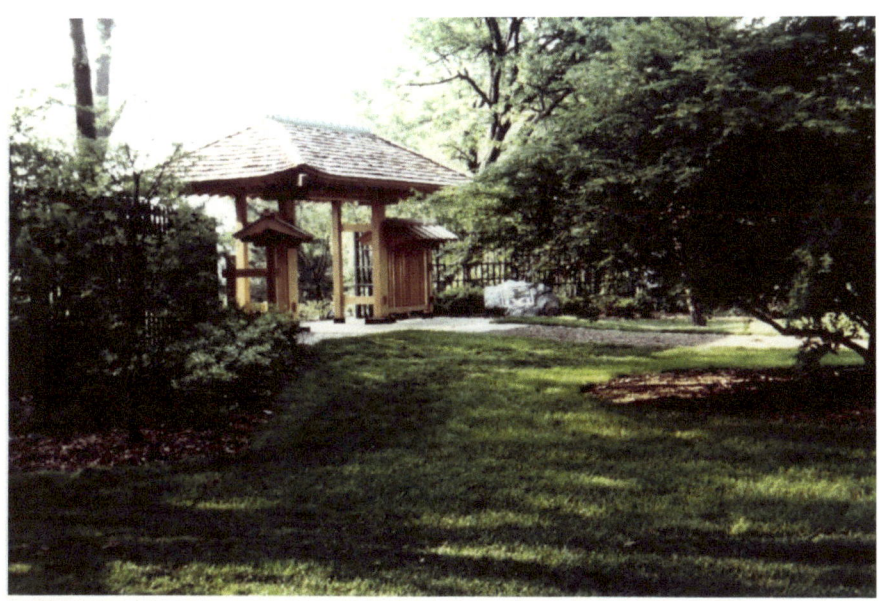

(Photo 07)

Linking the characteristics / images of the garden with the proposed definition needs to increase its usefulness and applicability in the development of design and management plans. Previous research has not fully explored this opportunity.

As is evident from the process of building the Manzanar National Historic Site in California State with a very important group of Japanese gardens and the process of formulating the management plan thereafter, the need for high quality definition in development and establishment is clear. Many experts and organizations are expressing interest in the Manzanar National Historic Site being designated as a World Heritage site. Having quality, effective and effective definition will increase the possibility of this deliberation.

It is very important to effectively define Japanese gardens in order to develop regional pride, communicate globally and to create, maintain and maintain gardens that support tourism not only in North America but also in Japan and the world It is important.

Chapter 6: Preceding Definition and Evaluation

Following lists some definition from surveys that this author identified and grouped them according to their professions and those found in dictionaries as examples..

(Table 10)

Developing definition

Group 1 :
Japanese Garden Professionals.

Respondent	Description
■ Makoto Suzuki	"Even though Takenosuke Tatsui, stated in 1991 , "that there is no firm definition of Japanese garden which strikes to the essence of Japanese garden, it is important to develop proper terminology and definition for Japanese garden, if one considers it as a subject of academic/scientific work." He does not offer a definition of Japanese (traditional) garden.
■ Yukio Yashiro	"Japanese Garden is truly in natural style while a western garden presents very formal man made organization as illustrated in Italian and French Garden. Contrasting to English Scenery (natural) Garden which presents a part of nature, the Japanese Garden is not just a copy of the nature but symbolization of the nature by use of plants, rocks, earth mound and water."
■ Makoto Nakamura	"Japanese garden is symbolic miniature garden in contrast to realistic scenery garden of England."

A complete list of survey is included in Appendix.

In order to evaluate these diverse definition statements, I developed a number of attribute as indicated below:

(Table 11)

Components:	Description:
1. Essence of the garden	Expression for imperial power in a vast Ground both for ceremonial, diplomatic and residential
2. Purpose and Use	It is a garden for palace and entertainment
3. Design Expression	Formal, axial, vista and symmetrical
4. Details: Facilities and Ornament	Water-Canal, pond and fountain Surrounded by tree Bosque

5. Spirituality and Symbolism	

In order to evaluate these preceding definition, I reviewed statements under study are reviewed to see if they have any linkage with attributes: Numbers 1,2,3,4,5 relate to those in the preceeding table. Following indicates occurrence of attributes from this study from Group 1 as an example.

(Table 12)

Evaluating definition

Group 1:
Japanese Garden Professionals.

Respondent	Description	Attribute
▪ Hiromasa Amasaki	It is nothing but a blending of grand nature's reincarnation and creative people's work.	1 5
▪ Osamu Mori	"… the special characteristics of the Japanese garden are in the ingenious artistry and symbolism which turn the miniature landscapes into something more profound and eternal."	1 5
▪ Teiji Ito	"…the Japanese garden is "a recreation of idealized nature" and "a kind of spatial art in outdoor environment."	1 5
▪ Seiko Goto	….lists four themes of Japanese gardens as follows: "The space to symbolize bigger nature by depicting beauty from its element….. The power of nature is a major theme…The second theme is its adaptation of features from other cultures, such as those of China and India…one of the distinguishing characteristics of the Japanese Garden is this reflection of multiple religious beliefs. The third theme is the representation of the natural scenery that appears in classical Japanese literature. The last theme is the tea ceremony…."".	1 2 3 5

(Table 13)

Tabulation

Evaluation Number	Attribute	
	Components:	Frequency out of thirty entries
1	Essence of the garden: Visual, Spatial and sensual	26 (30%): Group 1
2	Purpose and Use	11 (13%): Group 2
3	Design Expression	12 (15%): Group 2
4	Details: Facilities and Ornament	09 (11%): Group 2
5	Spirituality & Symbolism :	25 (30%): Group 1

Conclusion: controlling attributes are found to be those in Numbers 1 and 5.

A complete list of this evaluation is included in Appendix.

I have concluded that attributes could be grouped as:
* Group 1 as the Primary and
* Group 2 as the Secondary

Chapter 7: Image of the Japanese Garden

1. Image of the Japanese Garden

Linking characteristics/mental images of gardens with the proposed definition will enhance its utility and applicability in developing designs and management plans. No previous work has explored this opportunity in full. Fundamentals of sustaining Japanese gardens should be based in having professionals holding understanding of the significance, characteristics, technique and materials of Japanese gardens. The number of these professionals in North America is limited and fading. Concurrently, however, demand for the creation of quality Japanese gardens and fostering them has been expanding, as seen in the creation of new gardens in such places as Portland, Fargo, Vancouver, and Washington DC.

The amount of academic work on defining Japanese gardens applicable to North America is limited. Majority of them are found in Japanese and not in English. Today's social changes looking for more systematic and logical approaches and the information age of globalization requires that this situation to be amended not only in Japan but also and more so in the North America.

It is very significant to have an effective definition of Japanese gardens to create, preserve and maintain gardens that will promote developing local pride, communicating globally and supporting tourism not only in North America but also in Japan and the world.

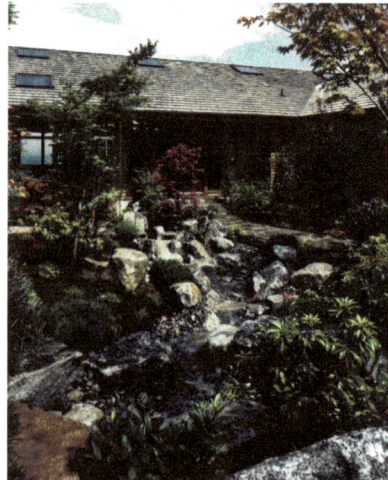

(Photo 08)

2. Research on existing literature

Takeo Uesugi noted about view of Japanese gardens described by Garrett Eckbo as follows: "He never neglected the concept of the Japanese garden either, but challenged the imitation of Japanese gardens in America. Among many people who were influenced by the Japanese gardens, Isamu Noguchi, Sculptor and Landscape Architect, should be noted as the best person who dedicated himself to contemporary arts by bringing the east together with the west." This author agrees with this view expressed by Eckbo on appreciating and understanding Japanese gardens. Another viewpoint is offered by Makoto Nakamura and Hiromasa Amasaki in "Creating Landscape", 2001, as: Evolution of Japanese Garden could be broken into three distinctive periods: Learning/Following Nature; Creating Nature and Returning to Nature; and Learning/Following Nature.

However, for people in North America, statements on or descriptions of Japanese gardens provided by such authors as Garrett Eckbo, Makoto Nakamura and Hiromasa Amasaki and James Rose to appreciate and understand Japanese Garden, included above, are probably too abstract and symbolic to be effective in use. This is due to confusion about the definition of Japanese garden as previously noted by Makoto Suzuki in 1996 in his study.

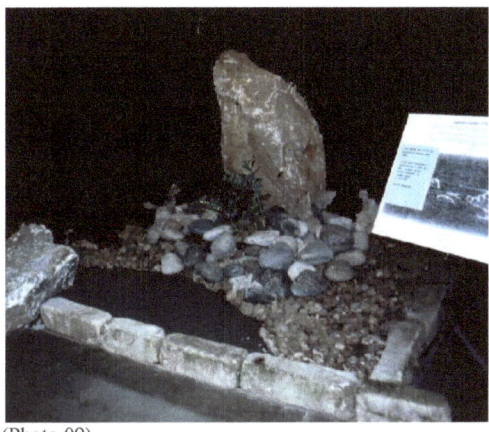

(Photo 09)

The following lists a number of other viewpoints by different authors about Japanese gardens: James Rose stated that "of course, you can have a real Japanese garden…all you have to do is be Japanese…". This thesis was started initially to counter the statement above by James Rose with an assumption that a development of simplified definition of Japanese gardens and the accompanying design method/process is possible.

Seiko Goto, with University of Nagasaki, responded that the Japanese garden is "The space to symbolize bigger nature by depicting beauty from its element." Dr. Makoto Nakamura, Professor Emeritus of Kyoto University, noted that "The Japanese garden is too complex to define it simply." However, he previously stated a "Japanese garden is symbolic miniature garden in contrast to realistic scenery garden of England."

Shinji Isoya wrote about Japanese gardens in "Gardens of Japan, 2005" as the following: "…Despite this diversity, gardens maintain the feeling of a Japanese garden. Then he questioned "why one can group these diverse gardens into one category under the term Japanese garden". He concluded by saying "the main reason for it exists in "appreciation of nature" and 'acceptance of nature as-is'.

Because these responses represent the both ends of the spectrum, it is clear that more systematic work should be done in defining Japanese gardens.

A number of the additional existing literature on Japanese gardens by such authors as Osamu Mori, Teiji Ito, Isoya Shinji and Makoto Suzuki have been researched. However most of the publications have not given a clear insight to questions of definition.,and they were written for Japanese readers only. The publications had not been well publicized and understood by people abroad.

To research further into the existing works in this area, the author reviewed a number of other publications, mostly in English and a limited number in Japanese. Authors of these publication are grouped into three categories of (1.) General Introduction and Illustration, (2.) History and Theory/Methodology, and (3.) Design-Practice. Authors of publications from categories (2.) and (3.) and containing words and phrases most relevant to the definition of Japanese gardens are selected as follows: Takeo Uesugi, James Rose, Makoto Nakamura, Amasaki, Hiromasa, Osamu Mori, Marc P. Keane, Koichi Kobayashi, Bruce Wiggigton, Yukio Yashiro, Seiko Goto, ,Norihisa Okada, David A Slawson, Johan Kraftner, Isoya Shinji, Marc P Keane, Makoto Suzuki, Teiji Ito, Kendall Brown, Norihisa, Takenosuke Tatsui, Kuitert Wybe, and Jeffery Burton. These are listed not in particular order.

Out of these publications, this author further screened them and selected the following authors' literature as representative of the existing works on a definition of Japanese gardens for further description and evaluation.

Statements or descriptions referring to a definition of Japanese gardens are summarized and evaluated on the basis of the following criteria: (1) Whether it is an effective statement in concise, simple, logical and clear manner as suitable for definition and (2) Whether it contains linkage with essence of Japanese garden as expressed in characteristics or mental images which are defined in the following section.

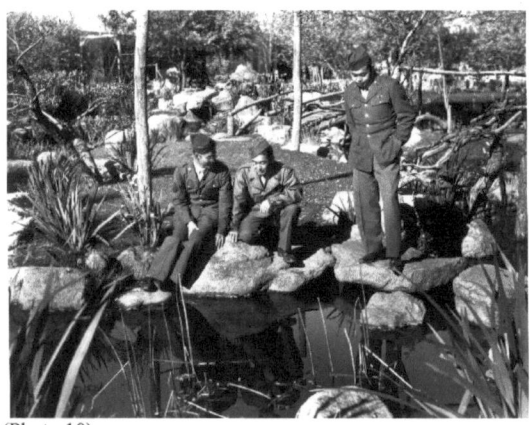

(Photo 10)

Techniques and materials employed in their writings are also listed as they should be an indication for their stating or referring to a definition of Japanese gardens.

2-1. Osamu Mori: Typical Japanese Garden, Shibata Publishing Co., 1962
2-1-1. Description of definition: Osamu Mori states that "… the Japanese garden, while based on natural scenery, is very much different in character from the Western version of landscape gardening. To make a capsule definition, the special characteristics of the Japanese garden are in the ingenious artistry and symbolism which turn the miniature landscapes into something more profound and eternal."
2-1-2. Technique and materials: The techniques and materials described include the following: Theme (style) of garden, including ponds and island, streams, fountains, waterfalls, Tsukiyama hills, Nosuji plains, Karesansui gardens, garden paths, stepping stones and flag stones, bridges, Buddhist garden structure, cottages, fences, hedges, garden gates, stone lanterns, water basins, trees and borrowed scenery.
2-1-3. Evaluation: It is an early attempt to define Japanese gardens expressed in English. It is in narrative and qualitative description and will be hard to be an effective definition. It does contain reference to natural scenery and the ingenious artistry and symbolism and miniature landscape as they relate to characteristics and images.

2-2. Teiji Ito, The Gardens of Japan, Kodansha Co., 1998
2-2-1. Description of definition: Teiji Ito describes Japanese gardens using two concepts: Nature Idealization and Microcosms. He elaborates those as stating that "…the Japanese garden is "a recreation of idealized nature" and "a kind of spatial art in outdoor environment."
2-2-2. Materials: Materials covered are: stone gathering, stone structures, stone groupings, stepping stones, gravel patterns, stone lanterns, fences and hedges, plants, moss and lawn, ponds and streams, fences and hedges.
2-2-3. Evaluation: Although not presented as a definition of the style, his description of Japanese gardens is based on two themes: nature and change in time. It is in essay form and is hard to be interpreted as a definition. No linkage to characteristics and images of Japanese garden is included.

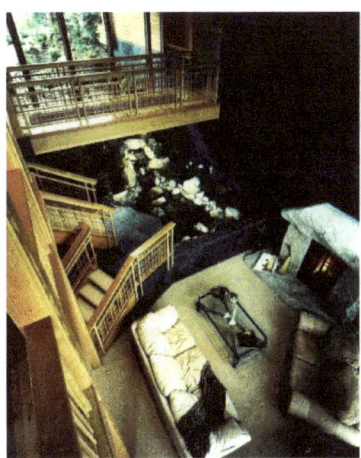

(Photo 11)

2-3. Seiko Goto and Takahiro Naka: Japanese Gardens--Symbolism and Design, Rutledge, 2016 and personal communication

2-3-1. Description of definition: Seiko Goto lists themes (which could be interpreted as contributing toward a definition) of Japanese gardens as follows: "The space to symbolize bigger nature by depicting beauty from its element….. The power of nature is a major theme…".
The second theme is its adaptation of features from other cultures, such as those of China and India, particularly Buddhism…. One of the distinguishing characteristics of the Japanese Garden is this reflection of multiple religious beliefs. The third theme is the representation of the natural scenery that appears in classical Japanese literature. The last theme is the tea ceremony….".
2-3-2. Technique: The following are listed: visual usage--lookout and borrowed scenery; physical usage--hills and plains.
2-3-3. Materials: The following are listed as elements: pond, river, mountain, waterfalls, island, rock, and built elements.
2-3-4. Evaluation: She offers a simple and concise statement, appropriate for a definition. She further offers four themes to support it: unique symbolism and objectives; power of nature; adaptation from other cultures; and the representation of the natural scenery. She does not indicate any linkage with characteristics and images of gardens.

2-4. Johann Kraftner: The Elegant Garden: Architecture and Landscape of the World's Finest Gardens, Rizzoli, Austria, 2012
2-4-1. Description on definition: Characteristics and Images
In describing Japanese gardens, Johann Kraftner stated that "… if European garden is a reflection of paradise expression of an imaginary order of the next world that appears to the various cultural and societal requirements, then the garden of the Far East in China and Japan is a reflection of nature of the country's own landscapes…. 'Spiritual' is the term often applied to describe the real meaning of Japanese gardens….".
2-4-2. Technique: He cites four underlying principles of tea ceremony –harmony, respect, purity and tranquility as they relate to gardens and tea houses.
2-4-3. Materials: He includes following principal materials: stone, gravel and sand, stepping stones, stone lanterns, water, moss and trees.
2-4-5. Evaluation: His writing does not conform to the style of a definition, however he offers "reflection of nature of the country's own landscapes..." and "Spiritual to describe the real meaning of Japanese gardens" as they could be interpreted as a part of a definition. He does not indicate any linkage with characteristics and images of garden, except "Spiritual".

2-5. Makoto Suzuki: The Image and View of Japanese Gardens in the Minds of Westerners, Tokyo Agricultural University, 1996
2-5-1. Description on definition: In deliberating on Japanese gardens, Makoto Suzuki states that "Even though Takenosuke Tatsui, stated in 1991 , "that there is no firm definition of Japanese garden which strikes to the essence of Japanese garden, it is important to develop proper terminology and definition for Japanese garden, if one considers it as a subject of academic/scientific work." Even though Suzuki classifies Japanese gardens into Japanese (traditional) gardens and Japanese-influenced gardens to minimize confusion, he does not offer a definition of Japanese (traditional) garden. No basis for evaluation is offered.

2-6. Yukio Yashiro, Characteristic of Japanese Art, Imanishi Publish, 1943
2-6-1. Description of definition: Yukio Yashiro describes Japanese gardens as "Japanese Garden is truly in natural style while a western garden presents very formal man made

organization as illustrated in Italian and French Garden. Contrasting to English Scenery (natural) Garden which presents a part of nature, the Japanese Garden is not just a copy of the nature but symbolization of the nature by use of plants, rocks, earth mound and water." Technique and materials are not covered.

2-6-2. Evaluation: As his work is on Japanese Art in general, Yashiro's description is also generalized except to offer that the Japanese garden is natural in style, and not just a copy but symbolization of nature. He does not indicate any linkage to characteristics and images except nature.

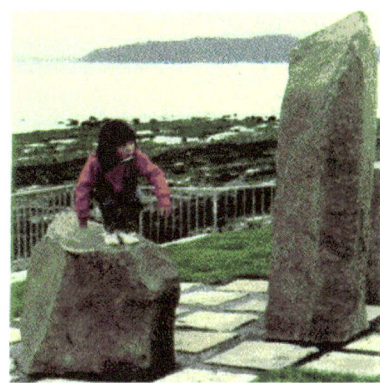

(Photo 12)

2-7. Makoto Nakamura, Characteristics of Japanese Garden Style, Kyoto College of Art, 1996

2-7-1. Description of definition: Nakamura states it as "Japanese garden is symbolic miniature garden in contrast to realistic scenery garden of England."

2-7-2. Evaluation: It is very simple and straightforward, but it differentiates Japanese gardens from other gardens of the world. His writing, despite the title, does not offer characteristics and images of Japanese gardens that this thesis is looking for.

2-8. Kendall Brown, Quiet Beauty: The Japanese Gardens of North America, Tuttle Publishing, 2013

2-8-1. Description of definition: Kendall Brown notes his interpretation of Japanese garden as follows: "… North American Japanese gardens are not merely translations, they are transformations calibrated to their time and place and interpreted through a social system that add complex layers of meaning." Book does not cover technique and materials.

2-8-2. Evaluation: It is a fairly good but general statement as a definition but is difficult to put to practical use. No linkages to characteristics and images are described.

2-9. Jeffery Burton on Garden Management Plan: Gardens and Gardeners at Manzanar, 2016

2-9-1. Description of definition: In producing this report, Jeffery Burton cited definitions stated by Osamu Mori, Seiko Goto, and Koichi Kobayashi and stated that "Manzanar's Japanese gardens certainly meet these definitions of a Japanese garden, in that they depict nature in miniature…". He further stated that these gardens were created in the most severe environment in contrast to most of the Japanese gardens in Japan. They are not recreation of surrounding environment as delivered in the Saku Tei Ki, but recollection of images of their homeland and familiar gardens.

2-10. Wikipedia.com

2-10-1. Description of definition: It defines Japanese garden as follows: Japanese gardens are traditional gardens that create miniature idealized landscapes, often in a highly abstract and stylized way.

2-11. Existing definition in Dictionaries

Following lists a number of definitions of Japanese garden as found in English language dictionaries today.

(1) "Iwanami Buddhism Dictionary" Kenkichi Ono: It is an outdoor space created for festival, ritual, entertainment, strolling, welcoming and other purposes under a set of special and seasonal aesthetic sense. Chiefly constructed with earth, stone, plants and water and generally associated with or incorporated with building. (2) "Britannica Encyclopedia": It is garden created directing toward formal (rock garden) and informal/natural garden based on unique set of attitudes toward nature and religion. (3) "Digital DaiJiSen": It is a general term for gardens created with unique Japanese technique. It is made mainly with natural materials and created to express nature in miniature and in symbolic form. (4) "Dai Ji Sen Dictionary": It is a Japanese style garden arranged picturesquely with pond, spring, plants, bridge, teahouse and other elements.

In concluding this section, following presents a definition of Japanese gardens as summarized from this section.

It is that Japanese garden is: (1) exhibiting the ingenious artistry and symbolism which turn the miniature landscapes into something more profound and eternal to idealize nature in gardens that give the impression of naturalness; (2) space to symbolize bigger nature by depicting beauty from its element";(3) a garden with unique symbolism and objectives that developed within a distinctive climate and culture; (4) a reflection of nature of the country's own landscapes.... "Spiritual" is the term often applied to describe the real meaning of Japanese gardens; (5) truly in natural style while western garden presents very formal man-made organization as illustrated in Italian and French gardens; (6).symbolic miniature garden in contrast to realistic scenery garden of England; (7)transformation calibrated to their time and place and interpreted through a social system; (8) traditional garden that creates miniature idealized landscapes, often in a highly abstract and stylized way; (9) a garden created through taking advantage of conditions of the site and symbolizing diversified natural scenery.

(Photo 13)

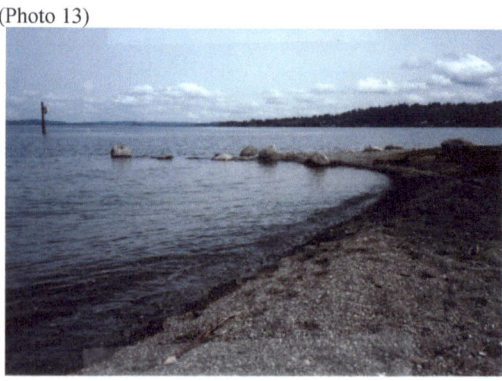

3. Identifying characteristics and images of Japanese garden

3-1. Comparative study on image of Japanese Garden.

This section compares findings from Makoto Suzuki's study in 1997 with surveys conducted by this author in 2004 and 2014 on images of Japanese gardens. Results from these surveys are compared in Table 1.

3-1-1. "The Image and View of Japanese Gardens in the minds of Westerners, 1997," Makoto Suzuki

Chapter Six of Suzuki's report covers "Study of degree of recognition of Japanese gardens by westerners residing in Japan." This study was based on showing a series of photos of Japanese gardens. As a summary of the study, it lists words most frequently associated with Japanese gardens.

3-1-2. "Survey conducted at the Fourth Symposium on International Japanese Gardens, 2004," by this author.

A request was sent to all 200 participants of the symposium to name their five most memorable Japanese gardens and cite their reasons for selection. No photographs were included in this survey. Over 30, mostly adult American professionals, replied.

5-1-3. "Survey conducted after the Second Annual Conference of North American Japanese Garden Association, 2014," by this author.

The following request was sent to more than 50 Japanese garden professionals and students in Japan. From reasons that respondents stated, the author considered them to be their images and view of the gardens in the following table. A sample photograph of seven gardens was included in this survey.

5-1-4. Result of Survey on the Image of Japanese Garden

Table 1 illustrates and compares the result of three surveys.

(Table 14) Result of surveys on image of Japanese garden compared

"The Image and View of Japanese Gardens in the minds of Westerners, 1997" Makoto Suzuki	" Survey at the Fourth Symposium of International Japanese garden, 2004" Koichi Kobayashi	" Survey at the second annual conference of North American Japanese garden Association, 2014." Koichi Kobayashi
peaceful, serene	Practical beauty, serenity	serenity
quiet	intimacy	serenity
simple	Zenness, sumie	sansui painting
green, peaceful, calm	Miniature, less	microcosm
natural	Naturalness	healing soul
formality	Majestic, amazing	
	spirituality	spirituality
	borrowed scenery	borrowed scenery
	Building & garden relationship	building & garden relationship
	history	history

Words presented in the table above in Suzuki's study came from westerners. Suzuki noted as a part of his study that Japanese, contrasting to selection by westerners, selected such words as pond, lantern, etc. which describe elements of gardens more. Words selected by westerners cover a more mental image they hold of Japanese gardens. Respondents of this author's survey were all Japanese of Japanese ancestry, but most of them had some level of familiarity and understanding of Japanese garden prior to the surveys. A comparison of Suzuki's and this author's survey yields the following result:

There are two levels of words most closely associated with Japanese garden. Level 1 consists of words presenting mental images: serenity, simplicity, intimacy, naturalness, spirituality and healing soul. Level 2 words describe the composition of gardens: for example, borrowed scenery, building and garden relationship and history.

3-2. Comparison of Degree of Recognition of Japanese Garden
"The Image and View of Japanese Gardens in the minds of Westerners, 1997", by Makoto Suzuki, is reviewed. In his writing, he started with defining the word "Japanese garden" and he studied the following: (1) how information on Japanese gardens was transmitted to westerners, (2) how westerners' views were formed and factors in forming views and images and (3) how Japanese gardens were recognized by westerners. He found that westerners' views of Japanese gardens included more mental states and sensitivity by stating quietness, greenery, peace, quietness and nature in contrast to cognitive image of such elements of Japanese garden composition as stone and pond by domestic Japanese respondents. This section additionally compares how people recognize Japanese garden, as exhibited in the following publications and a survey this author conducted.

3-2-1. Research on the existing literature
The following existing notable literature and sources are reviewed and compared:
A. "The Image and View of Japanese Gardens in the minds of Westerners," 1997, Makoto Suzuki: Most of the respondents are not garden professionals and some are not familiar with Japanese gardens.
B. "Gardens of Japan: Beginning," 2008, Norihisa Okada: Author listed gardens with deep personal association and affection.
C. "Gardens of Japan: Skill and craftsmanship and spirit," 2010, Shinji Isoya: Author tries to present the most representative Japanese gardens historically and geographically.
D. "Survey conducted at the second annual conference of North American Japanese Garden Association," 2014, Koichi Kobayashi: Most of the respondents are Japanese Garden Professionals from the western parts of Japan.
E. "Listing of Japanese Gardens" 2014, Internet website www.Japan-Guide.com: This site is oriented toward tourism.

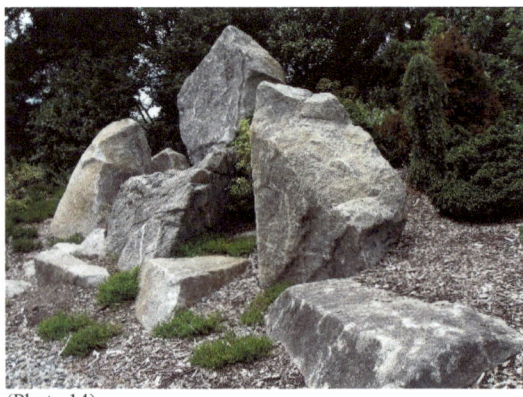
(Photo 14)

3-2-2. Result of the survey and comparison

I have been searching my soul to reach definition of essence of Japanese garden for some time.
And I realized that I have to come back to my starting point in to identify those gardens dear to me.

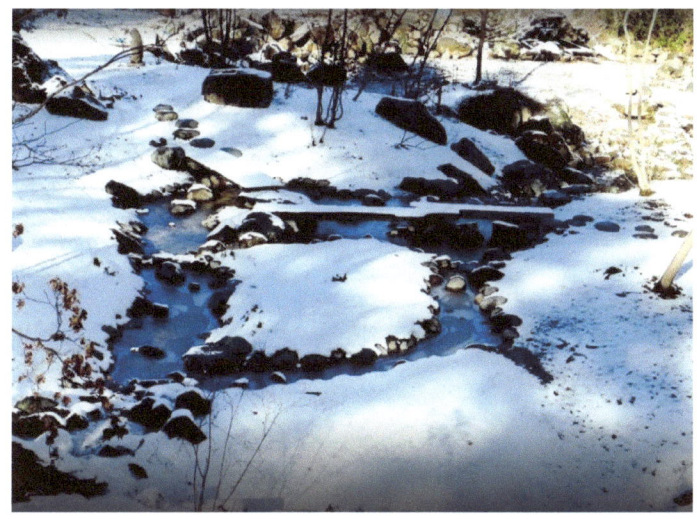

(Photo 15)

In identifying I used the following criteria:

Gardens which struck your heart
Gardens which moved your heart
Gardens which opens your eyes
Gardens which you remember most vividly
Gardens which you like to bring your loved ones to

Based on these, I came to the following:

KotoInn at DaitokuJi
SekisuiInn at KozanJi
RyoanJi
Hojo Garden at TofukuJi
Rock Work to KoInSan at SaihoJi
Moutsu Ji
A Garden in Toya by Naoe Suzuki

I would be very interested in knowing how you will determine yours.
Could you send me names of three to seven gardens having very essence of Japanese garden of these qualities?
Please attach any reason for pointing them if you could.

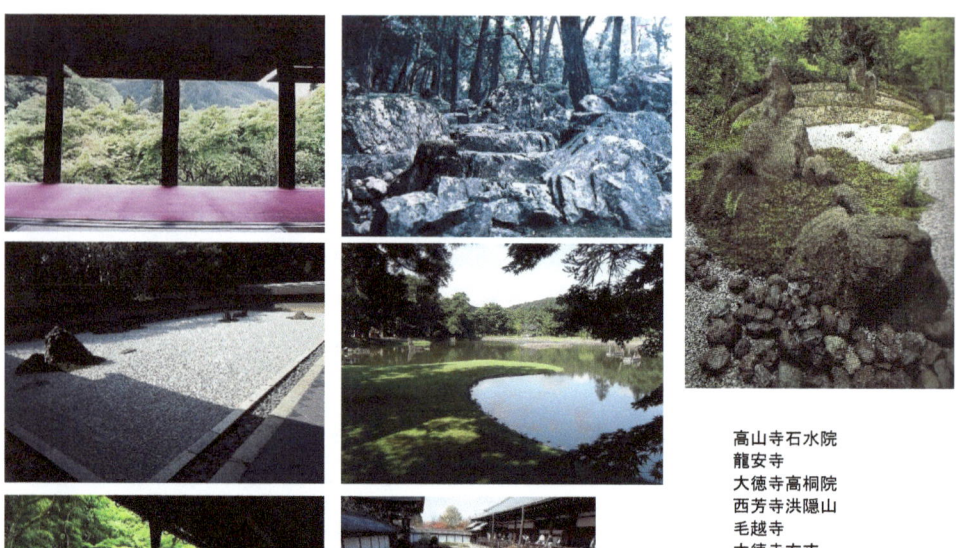

高山寺石水院
龍安寺
大徳寺高桐院
西芳寺洪隠山
毛越寺
大徳寺方丈
鳥谷の庭

(Photo 16)

The following gardens are cited as top 10-30 gardens by literature and sources listed above :

(Table 15) Highly rated Gardens

A. "The Image and View of Japanese Gardens in the minds of Westerners, 1997", Makoto Suzuki (listed in order of frequency)	B. "Gardens of Japan: Beginning, 2008 Norihisa Okada (list only pubic gardens, except Katsura and Shuugakuin)	C. "Gardens of Japan. Skill and craftsmanship and spirit" 2010 Shinji Isoya	D. " Survey conducted at the second annual conference of North American Japanese Garden Association, 2014." Koichi Kobayashi	E. "Listing of Japanese Gardens" 2014 www.Japan-Guide.com
Kinkaku Ji	Kinkaku Ji	Kinkaku Ji		
Ginkaku JI	Ginkaku JI	Ginkaku JI		
Ryuan Ji	Ryuan Ji	Ryuan Ji	Ryuan Ji	Ryuan Ji
Saihou Ji	Saihou Ji	Saihou Ji		Saihou Ji
Kanazawa kenrokuen		Kanazawa kenrokuen		Kanazawa kenrokuen
Katsura Rikyu	Katsura Rikyu	(Katsura Rikyu)	Katsura Rikyu	Katsura Rikyu
Hama Rikyu		Hama Rikyu		
Okayama Kourakuen		Okayama Kourakuen		
Koishigawa Kourakuen		Koishigawa Kourakuen		Koishigawa Kourakuen
Shuugakuin Rikyu	Shuugakuin Rikyu	(Shuugakuin Rikyu)		
Takamatsu Ritsurin	Takamatsu Ritsurin		Takamatsu Ritsurin	Takamatsu Ritsurin
Daitoku Ji Daisenin	Daitoku Ji Daisenin	Daitoku Ji		Daitoku Ji Daisenin

The following famous gardens are also cited. Highlighted gardens are cited more than twice in respective surveys.

(Table 16) Gardens cited secondarily

B. "Gardens of Japan:Beginning, 2008 Kazuhisa Okada (list only pubic gardens, except Katsura and Shuugakuin)	C. "Gardens of Japan: Skill and craftsmanship and spirit" 2010 Shinji Isoya	D. " Survey conducted at the second annual conference of North American Japanese Garden Association, 2014."Kobayashi
Byodou In	Byodou In	
Murin An	Murin An	
Shikunshi En		Shikunshi En
Gardens:Mirei Tsukino Katsura	Tsukino Katasura	
Gardens:Fukaya Keio Plaza	Shukkei En	Shukkei En
Koho An		Koho An
	Moutsu Ji	Moutsu Ji
	Zuihou In	
Tea Garden :Iida	Yosui En	KoGosho
Kyoto M. Art	Shiramizu Amida Dou	Budda In
	Shirakawa Nanko	
YorouTenmei Hantenchi	Mito Kairaku En	Koyou In
Shomyou Ji	Rikugi En	Sanzen in
Eihou Ji	MukoJima HyakkaEn	Sentou Gosho
Kitabatake Clan	Shiba Rikyu	Sankei En
Kyuu ShuuRin Ji	Kiyomizu Garden	Entsuu Ji
Asakura Clan	Kyu Furukawa	Shosei En
Konchi In	Shinjyuku Gyoen	Tairyu Sansou
Tohgu In	Gyokudo Bijyutsu	Kayu Sou
Jyoruri Ji	Jyoju In	Kohto In
	Suizenji Koen	
	Iso Teien	
	Shikina En	
	Daitokuji Hojyou	
	Nijyo Ninomara	

3-2-3. Findings and Conclusion of this section

This comparison is made to identify if there are any common threads among those cited by different individuals and agencies. Common threads may exist in: most frequently cited garden, common garden style, common garden design vision or composition, common aesthetic characteristics and common abstraction quality. As the conclusion, the following gardens are most commonly and frequently listed:
KinkakuJi, GinkakuJi, RyoAnJi, SaiHoJi, Kanagawa Kenrokuen, Katsura Rikyu, Hama Rikyu, Okayama KorakuEn, Koishikawa Korakuen, ShuuGakuinRikyu, Takamatsu Ritsurin Koen, DaitokuJi DaisenIn. And secondarily ByouDouIn, Murian An, Shikunshi En, Tsukino KatsuranoNiwa, Side Garden at KeioPlaza and Koho An.

3-3. Exploring linkage between gardens and their mental images
3-3-1.Linkage between gardens and mental images.
First based on gardens frequently listed in a number of publications and
surveys, and images (words) identified, an attempt is shown to seek linkages between them in solid line in the following table. Second, this linkage identification is further supplemented by this author in dashed line on the same table. And finally type of garden style associated with this identification is presented. From this table, it is evident that most of the gardens with a distinctive image are associated with pond/hill and tea garden as their feature theme.

(Table 17) Identification of linkages among garden, their characteristics and features, supplemented and final identification

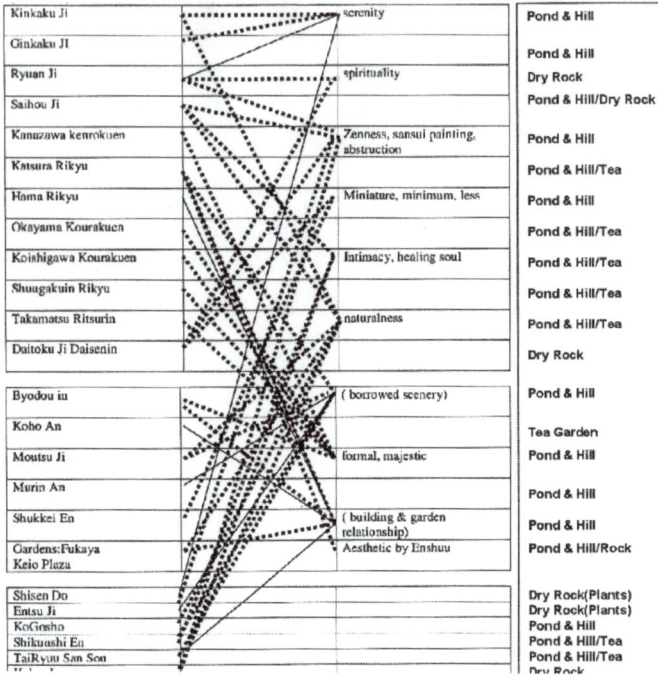

Based on findings as above, this author establishes gardens with pond and hill features to be the basis for developing a definition.

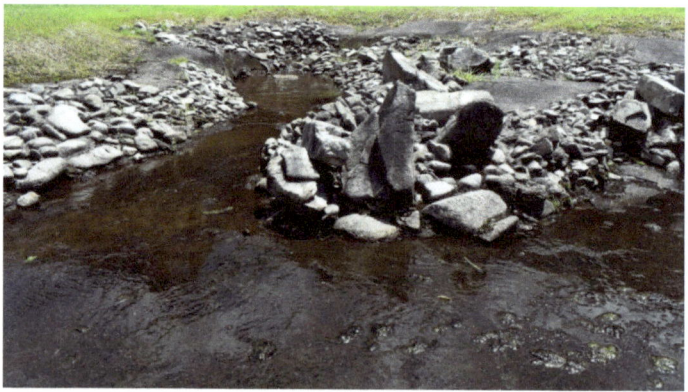

(Photo 17)

6. Developing and Evaluating the Definition

This section is developing an appropriate definition based on the preceding findings will be evaluated based for its utility.

Seiko Goto noted that complicating the definition of Japanese gardens outside of Japan is the fact that different styles have been popular at different times. The Japanese daimyo garden of the Edo period was the first celebrated garden style outside of Japan; minimalist gardens were largely ignored by Western scholars and dry gardens did not become well-known to Americans until the United States military occupied Japan after World War II. Another complicating issue is pointed out by Wybe Kuitert of Seoul University in 2002: Japanese gardens outside Japan often have many different elements in a single garden.

Summarizing the preceding studies, definitions listed above are reviewed to see if they meet the following attributes needed for defining Japanese gardens: characteristics/mental image, design method, and materials., Characteristics/ images covers: serenity, simplicity, intimacy, naturalness, spirituality and healing soul. Design method focuses on spatial formulation through the use of dynamic asymmetrical balance and borrowed scenery, and Materials focuses on natural materials.

The author further analyzes and refines the following definitions of Japanese gardens by others as to whether they meet the criteria for definition, as described above:
(1) It is a garden that reflects nature in the country's own landscapes,
(2) It is a garden that symbolizes greater nature by depicting beauty from its elements,
(3) It is a garden that possesses objectives that developed within a distinctive climate and culture,
(4) It is a garden that creates miniature idealized landscapes, often in a highly abstract and stylized way,
(5) It is a garden that gives the impression of naturalness different from gardens presenting very formal manmade organization as illustrated in Italian and French Garden,
(6) It is a symbolic miniature garden in contrast to realistic scenery garden of England,
(7) It is a garden exhibiting spirituality in describing the real meaning of Japanese gardens
And (8) It is a garden to show transformation calibrated to their time and place and interpreted through its social system.

The author believes a Japanese garden must be a created space where people will be engulfed by nature, leading them to deep personal contemplation. Contrasted with Western style gardens, the Japanese garden has characteristics which lead the visitor to appreciate nature, history and artistry.

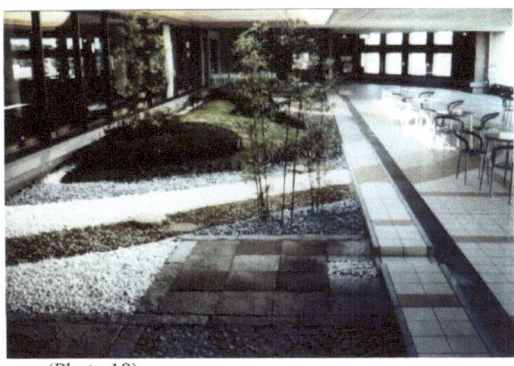

(Photo 18)

Based on preceding definitions by others and studies presented in this paper, this author proposes the following three versions as the definition of the Japanese Garden with a refinement by including North American sensitivities toward environmental factors, healing properties and interplay with the natural world.

Version 1: It is the garden incorporating symbolism from ancient sources, designs which foster peace and serenity by relying on natural elements. Version 2: It is the garden using miniature idealized landscapes to form a potent combination of abstract and stylized designs often in informal/natural way with asymmetry and .Version 3: It is the garden celebrating the Japanese attitude and reverence of nature by engaging the visitors in a natural setting, using natural elements. The natural garden transports visitors to higher realms of consciousness: meditating, praying, healing, refreshing and pleasure.

In conclusion, the author wishes that respective gardeners and garden managers review this proposal for its utility in updating management plans and through necessary modification, adopt it as a part of their own management plan.

In addition to the definition, the designer must be guided by the following principles of design: one should compose the landscape with a deep understanding of the purpose of the garden and respect for creative and innovative ideas. One should create this landscape composition which represents the natural coast, deep mountains and streams. Natural materials as earth, water, rocks and plants which fit the local environment will be utilized. Manmade structures such as a stone lantern could be added as an accent in the landscape. The garden must be fostered and maintained with a deep understanding of its ecological basis and artistic foundation.

Chapter 8: Is there boundary for Japanese Garden?

We often discuss about Japanese Garden without a clear idea of sphere or boundary. Following attempts to illustrate an answer to this question by a simple diagram for further discussion.

One could adopt this boundary as long as one clealy define it in discussing. I propose the boundary shown in double frame to be the one.

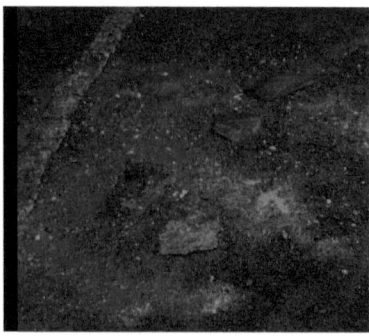

(Photo 19)
(Figure 09)

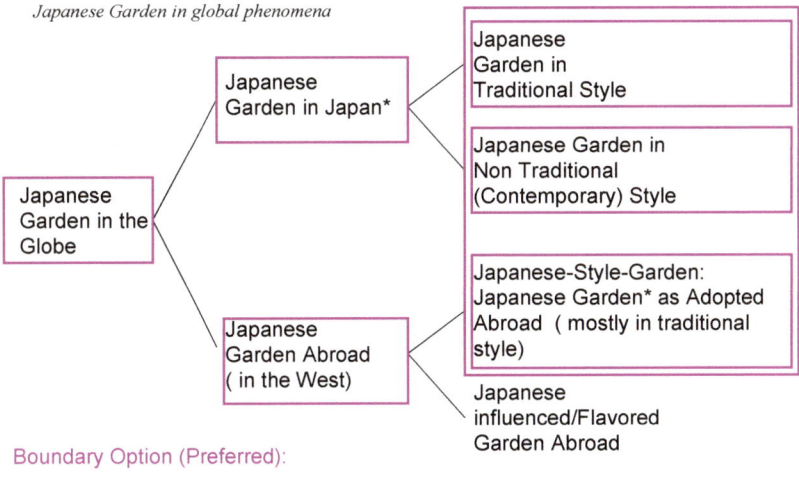

Mokoto Suzuki proposed use of terminology for describing (defining) Japanese Garden as presented in the table below. He has yet to proclaim definition for the Japanese Garden.

(Table 18) Reprint from JILA Journal

表1-1 「日本庭園」の学術用語法（鈴木　誠，1993／1996改訂）

作庭地	作庭者	庭　園　形　式	学術用語使用例	通　俗　的　用　語　使　用　例
日本国内	日本人	日本の伝統的形式	日本式庭園	日本庭園，日本式庭園，日本の庭園
		日本の伝統的形式外　特定形式なし	日本庭園（又は作品名）	日本の庭，和風庭園，和風の庭
	外国人	日本の伝統的形式	日本式庭園　日本風庭園	
		日本の伝統的形式外　特定形式なし	作品名	○○（国名）庭園　作品名
日本国外	日本人	日本の伝統的形式	日本式庭園　日本庭園	日本庭園　和風庭園
		日本の伝統的形式外　特定形式なし	作品名	作品名
	外国人	日本の伝統的形式	日本式庭園　日本風庭園	日本庭園　和風庭園
		日本の伝統的形式外　特定形式なし	作品名	○○（国名）庭園　作品名

（注）この用語法（案）では，作庭の時代規定（古庭園，伝統的庭園，歴史的庭園，史的庭園）と，庭園の価値・性格規定（名勝庭園，日本のにわ）は問わない。

Chapter 9 : Overviews of Japanese Garden for the Future

1. Overviews of Japanese Garden for the Future

Following table indicates my current overviews of Japanese garden to be projected to the future to help identify the World and Sphere.

(Figure 10)

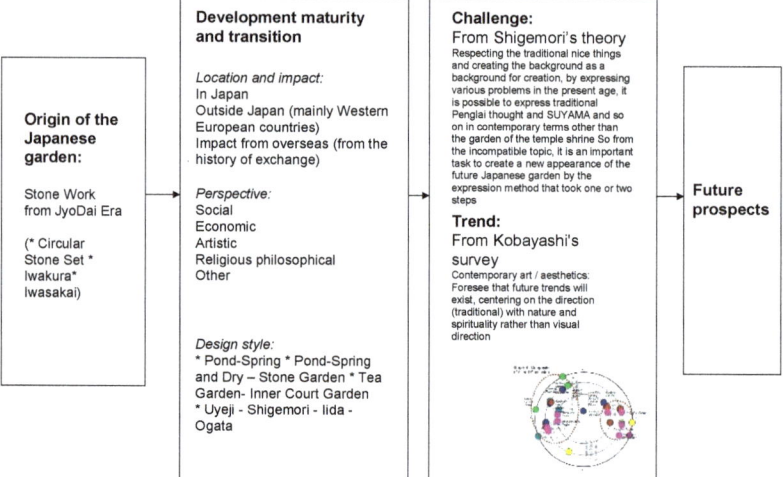

Overview of Japanese Garden for the Future (preliminary)

2. Predicting Future Trend

Following diagram attempts to illustrate "Predicting Future Trend" based on a number of publication by such authors as Norihisa Okada, Kendall Brown and others. Complete survey is included in Appendix.

Diagrams are produced as follows:

- On vertical axis; it shows two major orientations: On the top, Therapeutic and Biophilic and at the bottom, Ecological and Biological
- On horizontal axis; it shows two major garden form, Traditional and Modern (Geometric).

Individual studies are made into composite to reveal the overall projection.

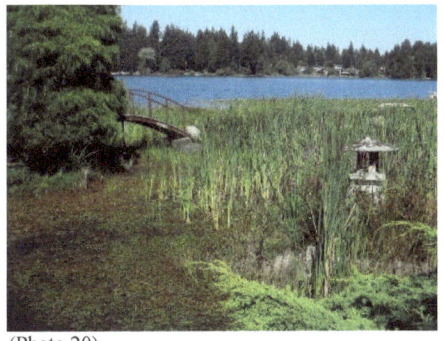
(Photo 20)

(Figure 11)

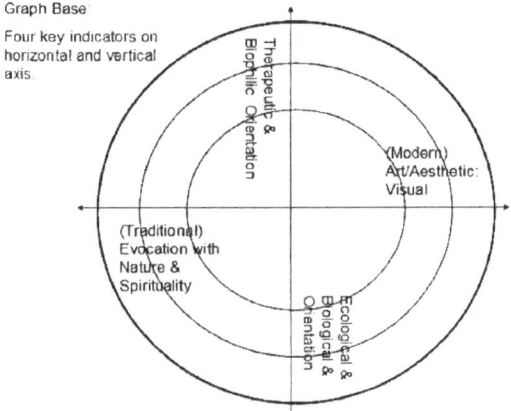

(Figure 12 & 13)

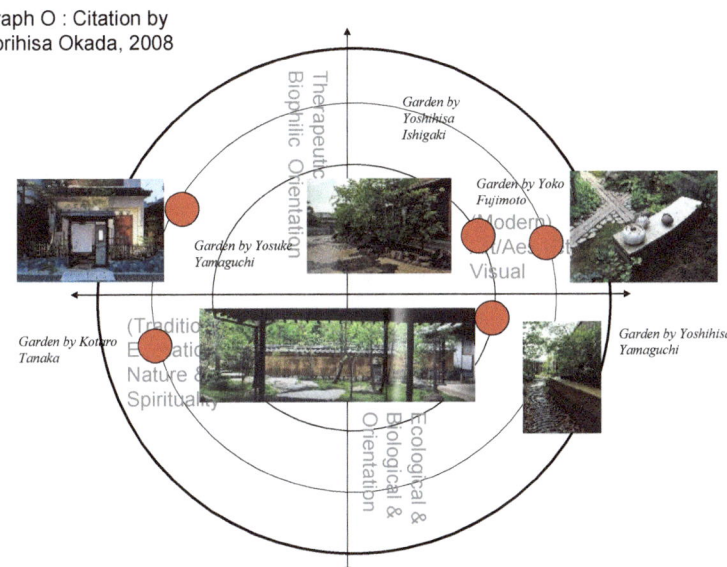

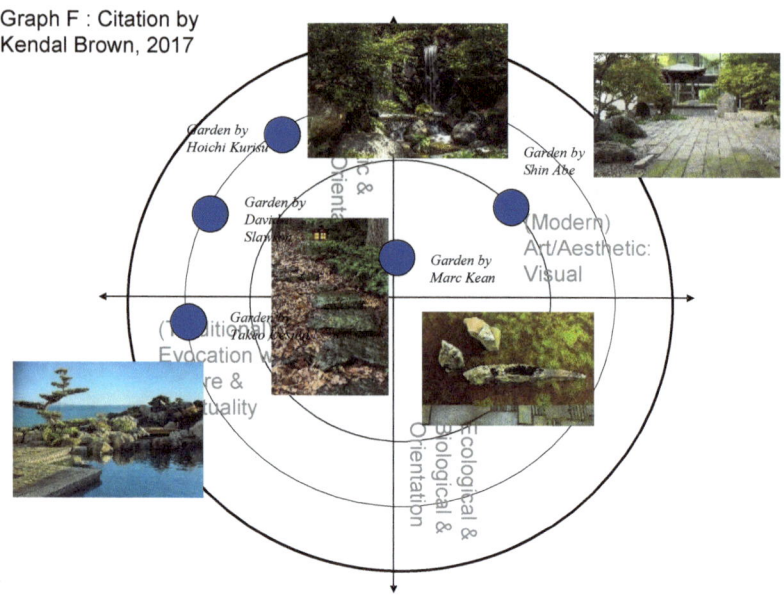

(Figure 14)

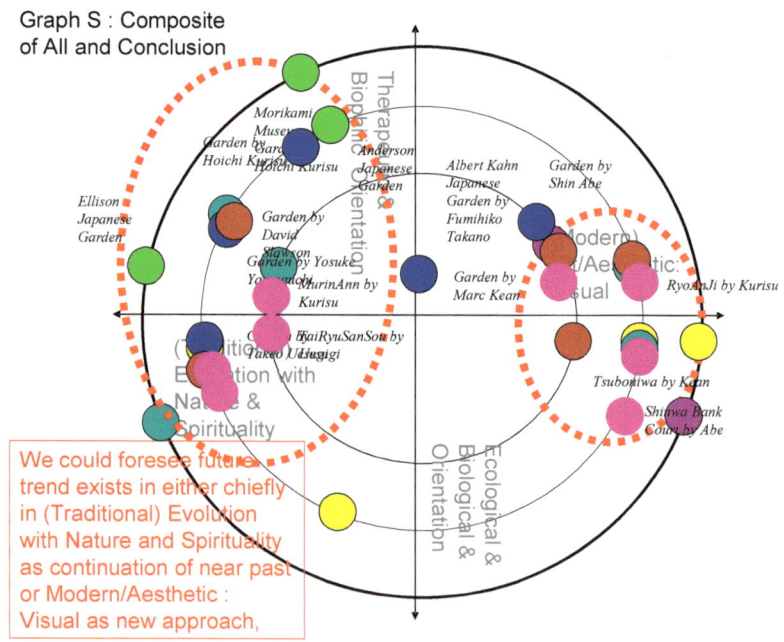

We could foresee future trend exists in either chiefly in (Traditional) Evolution with Nature and Spirituality as continuation of near past or Modern/Aesthetic : Visual as new approach,

Throughout the course of this study, I have begun to realize there could be a series of garden elements which could be iconic replacing bright colored torii gate, strange stone lanterns and bridges to name a few. I am advocating the following elements could overtake previous ones.

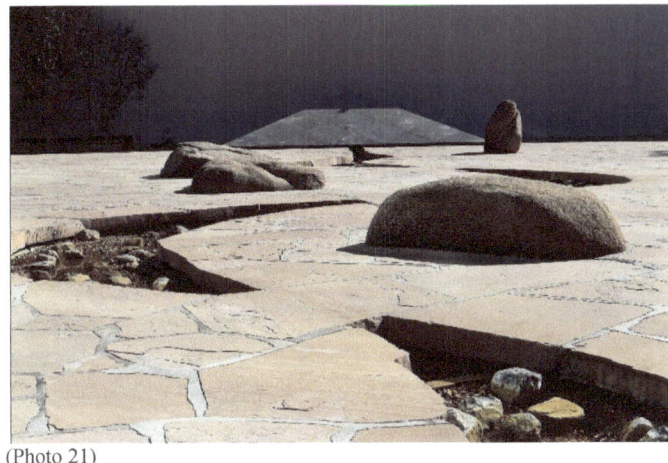

(Photo 21)

(Figure 15-18)

Future Trend in a global phenomena of Japanese Garden:
Stone wall as a major element in the garden

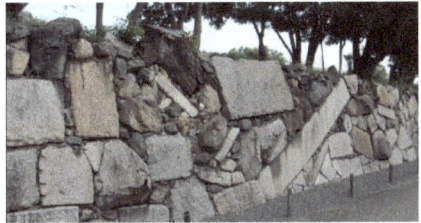

ShoSeiEnn, Kyoto (Edo Period)

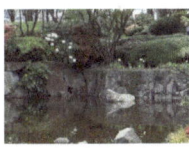

Momiji Garden, Vancouver, 1993

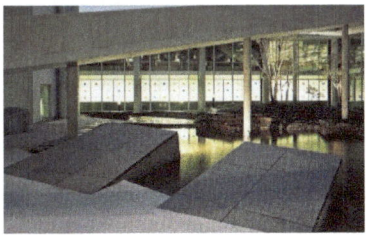

Belgen University Court, 2001

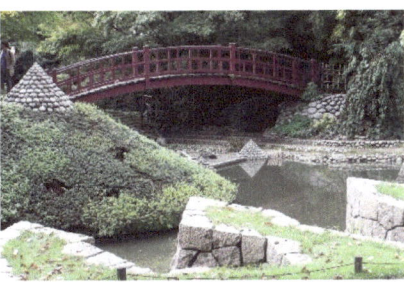

Albert Kahn Japanese Gaarden, 1988

Courtyard at Portland Japanese Garden, 2017

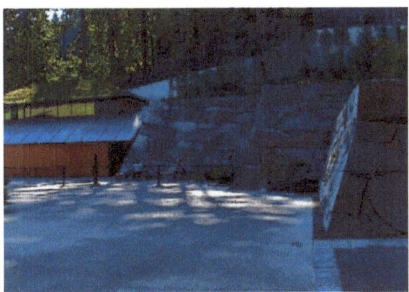

Future Trend in a global phenomena of Japanese Garden:
Stone wall as a major element in the garden

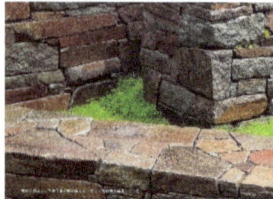

By Takusue Yoneyama

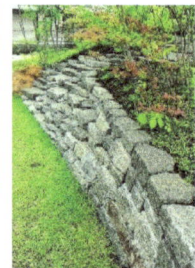

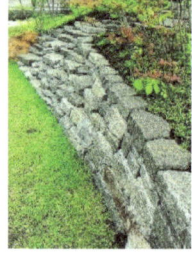

Wall by Hiroshi Terashita

Wall by Yuji Yamada

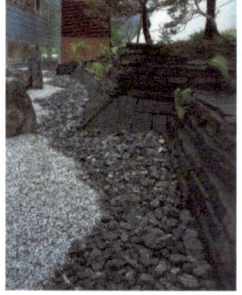

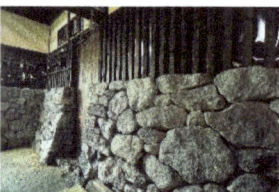

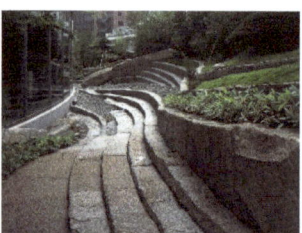

Belgen University Court, 2001

Wall by Hidetomo Obata

Cerulean Tower Tokyu Hotel, 2001

Future Trend in global phenomena of Japanese garden:
Tile Paving as a major element in the garden

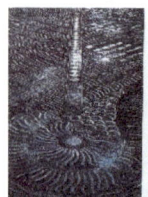
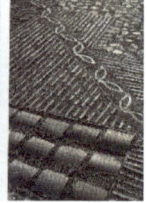

By Kaz Izue

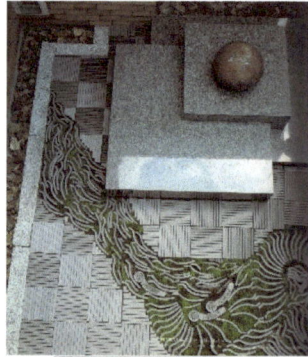

By Norihisa Okada

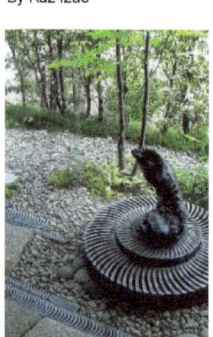

By Yoko Tai

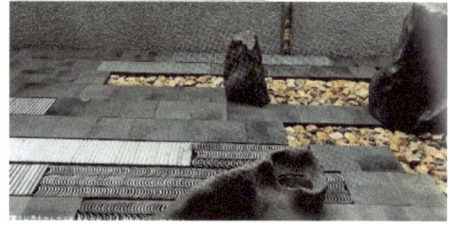

Future Trend in a global phenomena of Japanese Garden:
Contemporary Tsubo Niwa Garden as a major element in the garden

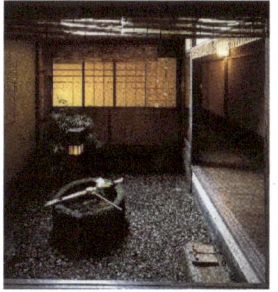

By Osamu Ishii
By Yasujiro Aoki

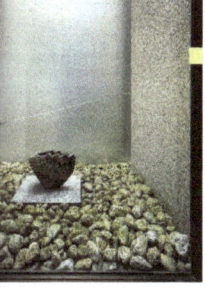

By Kazumasa Ohira

By Yoshinobu Kubo

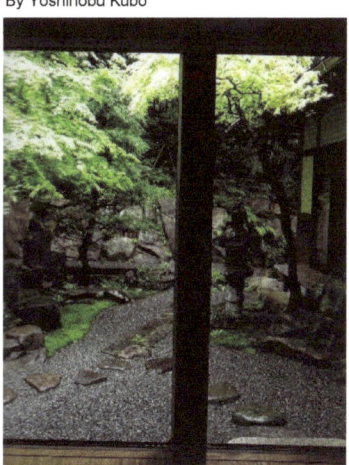

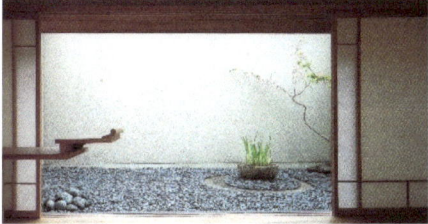

Chapter 10 : Qualification in Definition

Based on preceding studies, I am proposing the following components for developing definition of Japanese Garden.

Definition of Japanese Garden shall describe:
1. Essence and Image of the garden: visual, spatial and sensual
2. Attitude of Japanese toward nature in spiritualism and symbolism

And secondarily describe:
3. Purpose and Use
4. Design Expression
5. Details

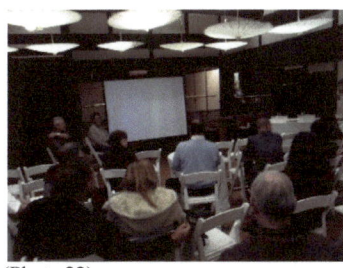

(Photo 22)

Chapter 11: Definition Proposed

Let us call gardens which lead mankind to enduring Japanese history and culture and also which reminds you of the nature providing serenity, tranquility, peacefulness and spirituality as the "Japanese Garden".

(Table 19)

Version No.	Included component	Statement	Word count
Version One	Essence of the garden: Visual, Spatial and sensual	Japanese garden is a space where there is a sense of connection to the cosmos, universe and eternity.	84
Version Two	Essence of the garden: Visual, Spatial and sensual Purpose and Use	Japanese garden is a space where there is a sense of connection to the cosmos, universe and eternity. The Japanese garden is A space where there is a sense of recalling natural landscape and changing of time. A space where there is a linkage to Japanese culture and history. A space where there is a sense of connectedness to the cosmos, universe and eternity.	297
Version Three	Essence of the garden: Visual, Spatial and sensual Purpose and Use Design Expression Details	Japanese garden is a space where there is a sense of connection to the cosmos, universe and eternity. The Japanese garden is A space where there is a sense of recalling natural landscape and changing of time. A space where there is a linkage to Japanese culture and history. A space where there is a sense of connectedness to the cosmos, universe and eternity.	461

| | | A combination of stationary and sequential organization, with symmetrical, natural and non axial layout, and employing traditional design method and technique and mostly natural materials. | |

References:
1. Katahira, Miyuki "Image of Japanese Gardens in the West and The Gardens of Japan according to Jiro Harada," Metropolitan Asian Art Research Center,
2. Condor, Joshua, "The Art of the Japanese Gardening in Japan", R. Meiklejohn & Co., 1886
3. Harada, Jiro, "The Gardens of Japan" The Studio Limited, 1928
4. Makoto Suzuki, The Image and View of Japanese Gardens in the Minds of Westerners, Journal of Landscape Architecture, Tokyo Agricultural University, 1997
5. Brown, Kendall, Japanese Influenced Garden, Rizzoli, 1991
6. Wybe, Kuitert, Themes in the History of Japanese Garden Art, University of Hawaii, 2002
7. Seiko Goto: Japanese Gardens--Symbolism and Design, Routledge-Taylor and Francis Group, 2016
8. Uesugi, Takeo, International Japanese Garden Symposium Proceeding; View on Japanese Garden, Seattle 2001
9. Eckbo, Garrett, Landscape We See, McGraw
10. Nakamura, Makoto and Amasaki, Hiromasa, Creating Landscape, Showado Publisher, Kyoto, 2001 and , Characteristics of Japanese Garden Style, Kyoto College of Art, 1996
11. Rose, James, Garden Makes Me Laugh, Silvermine Publisher. New York 1965
12. Mori, Osamu, Typical Japanese gardens, Shibata Co. 1962
13. Ito, Teiji (trans. Ralph Fiedrich & Masajiro Shimamura), Space and Illusion in the Japanese Garden, Weatherhill & Tankosha, 1973.
14. Shinji, Isoya, Gardens of Japan: Skilled Craftmanship and Spirit, Chuuo Shinsho, Tokyo, 2010
15. Kobayashi, Koichi, Legacy of Seattle Japanese Garden: Proceeding of the International Japanese Garden Symposium, 2001, and Monograph, Academia.edu 2015
16. Wiggigton, Bruce, Study of Japanese Garden, Marrietta College, Pennsylvania, 1963
17. Yashiro,Yukio, Charachteristics of Japanese Art, Imanishi, 1943
18. Okada, Norihisa, From Garden to City and Back Again to Garden, Japan, 1999
19. Slawson, David, The secret teachings in the art of Japanese Gardens: Design principles, Kodansha int. 1987
20. Kraftner, Johan, Architecture and Landscape of the World's Finest Gardens, Austrie, 201
21. Keane, Marc P, Japanese Garden Design, Tuttle Publishing, 1996.
22. Takei, Tatsunosuke, Periodical Thought on Japanese Garden
23. Jeffery Burton, Manzanar Japanese Garden Management Plan, National Park Service, 2016.

24. Tagsold, Christian, Space in Translation, University of Pennsylvania Press, 2017
25. Kawai, Noriko, A Monograph on the Possible Growth of Real Estate Market of the High Quality Japanese Residences with Japanese Gardens Regarding Globalization, JILA Journal 2017

Photo Credits:

1. Photographed by Kobayashi: Seattle Arboretum Japanese Garden
2. By Bitcoin Club
3. Designed and Photographed by Kobayashi: Bodine Residence Garden
4. Photographed by Kobayashi:Seko Garden and Seminar
5. Photographed by Kobayashi
6. Photographed by Kobayashi: Moutsuji Temple Garden
7. Designed and Photographed by Kobayashi: Osaka Garden in Chicago
8. Designed and Photographed by Kobayashi: Smith Residence Garden
9. Designed and Photographed by Kobayashi: Seattle Center
10. Archive by Manzanar National Historic Site
11. Designed and Photographed by Kobayashi: Smith Res Garden
12. Designed and Photographed by Kobayashi: Seattle Alki Beach Park
13. Designed and Photographed by Kobayashi: Lake Washington Shore
14. Designed and Photographed by Kobayashi: Kubota Garden Forecourt
15. Photographed by Kobayashi: Kakushoji Temple
16. Photographed by Kobayashi
17. Photographed by Kobayashi: Jyonokoshi Iseki
18. Designed and Photographed by Kobayashi: Fukuhara University Plaza Garden
19. Designed and Photographed by Kobayashi: Osaka Garden in Chicago
20. Photographed by Kobayashi: Seko Garden
21. Photographed by Kobayashi: California Scenario
22. Photographed by Kobayashi: Seminar at Hakone Garden

Appendix:

Appendix I: Attitude on Developing Definition of Japanese Garden

Together with personal communications and a number of workshops as listed below have been held to discuss need and significance for defining Japanese garden:

Workshop 1. Bellevue with non professional and long time residents of USA
Workshop 2. Seattle with non professional American with Japanese garden experience
Workshop 3. Vancouver with Professional Japanese Gardeners
Workshop 4. Tokyo with professional Japanese landscape architects (coming)
Workshop 5. Kyoto with professional gardeners (coming)

Questionnaire 6. Responses from European designers, researchers, writers and garden lovers.

This report is a summary from these workshops and questionnaires..

This report is a draft of inventory and analysis for your view.
Please review and correct as you find needed.

Group A: Off shore Non Japanese designers with experiences in Japan					
Negative		Neutral		Positive	
	David Sloawson, USA				
Marc Kean, USA					
		J.Skuba, USA			
Graham Hardman					
			Kendall Brown, USA		
					Edzard Teubert, Canada
			Ken Lamb, Australia		
			Don Chamberlain, USA		
			Oliver Geslin, France		
			Cristian Tagsold, GE		
			Carla Amorim, Spain		

Group B: Off shore Japanese designers in Canada					
Negative		Neutral		Positive	
					Imashimizu
					Ogawa
					Izawa
					Wakino
					Kaneda

					Ryo Sugiyama
					Kengo Sakai
					Ashizawa
					Hirokazu Okusa
					Shinpei Okada

Group C : American Non Garden Professionals					
Negative		Neutral		Positive	
			Patii Brown, USA		
			Connie Croy, USA		
			Tony Monk, USA		
			Cindy Pierce, USA		
					Ken Graff, USA

Group D : Japanese Non Garden Professionals In USA					
Negative		Neutral		Positive	
		Junko Akagi			
		Hiromi Komatsu			
		Tsutomu Sasaki			
		Mariko Maita			
		Hideaki Kawachi			

Group E : Off shore designers in Europe					
Negative		Neutral		Positive	

			Arien Tuin (NL)	
			Denis Bour (USA in JP)	
			Ian Fleming, UK	
			Tom Magielsen, NL	
	AKA Melvyn Westreich (ISRAEL)			
			Nadia Vasileva, ES	
			Daijiro Mizuno, UK	
			Maria Tor, ES	
			Mario Cardano Mrtinez, ES	
			Javier Vives Riego, ES	

Group X; Summary				
Negative		Neutral		Positive

	David Sloawson, USA			
Marc Kean, USA				
		J.Skuba, USA		
Graham Hardman, UK				
			Kendall Brown, USA	
				E.Teubert, Canada
		K. Lamb, Australia		
			D. Chamberlain, USA	
			Oliver Geslin, France	
			Cristian Tagsold, GE	
			Carla Amorim,	

				Spain	
				Imashimizu	
				Ogawa	
				Izawa	
				Wakino	
				Kaneda	
				Ryo Sugiyama	
				Kengo Sakai	
				Ashizawa	
				Hirokazu Okusa	
				Shinpei Okada	

			Junko Akagi		
			Hiromi Komatsu		
			Tsutomu Sasaki		
			Mariko Maita		
			Hideaki Kawachi		

				Arien Tuin (NL)	
				Denis Bour (USA in JP)	
				Ian Fleming, UK	
				Tom Magielsen, NL	
		AKA Melvyn Westreich (ISRAEL)			

				Nadia Vasileva, ES	
				Daijiro Mizuno, UK	
				Maria Tor, ES	
				Mario Cardano Mrtinez, ES	
				Javier Vives Riego, ES	

Responses on the need/significance on definition

Group Z : Con/Against/Neutral
Offshore designers with Japanese experience

Respndent	Description
Marc Kean, USA	My honest answer is that I do not think it is necessary to attempt to define what a Japanese garden is. Not from my point of view as a designer in any case. I also do not think it is possible to truly define what a Japanese garden is.
David Sloason, USA	To be honest, I don't see a need for exploring the definition of Japanese Gardens. What good would it do? Seeking such a definition does not engage the student in experiential learning and therefore is a waste of time.
Christian Tagsold, Germany	I think definitely yes but only to find out what people think, not to develop a better or even perfect definition which in my opinion is futile.
Ken Brown, USA	I agree with Christian that a single definition of Japanese garden is not very helpful. Perhaps Christian ad I are raised in the academic environment that says that almost all meanings are contingent, open to change based on context and over time.

Responses on the need/significance on definition

Group A : Neutral
Offshore designers with Japanese experience

Respondent	Description
Jerome Skuba	…… I can only offer you my opinion and understanding as a contemporary man of the West. Regarding this vexing topic, As I understand the quest for a universal definition of what is a Japanese Garden, *Nihon teien* is elusive at best. What do I mean by this? Seeing and Understanding are inseparably linked together to gain some sense of the "What is" that! It is a universal that is understood yet undefinable in words. It is, in my mind, comprehending something that resides in the subconscious, that becomes conscious when seen through the eyes. It is a feeling that resonates with ones intuition and deep memory. ……… We know it when we see it, there are no words that can define it except one. It is Essence: something understood deeply within every person, it is of ancient origins as rediscovered residual memories lost in time. Maybe it could also be defined as *Enso*.

Responses on developing definition

Group C : Pro/For/ Neutral for Definition
American non professional Japanese gardeners

Respondent	Description
Patii Bower, USA	Very groomed - precise. Beauty, serenity, peace, reflection, and tailored
Connie Croy, USA	Options, geometric, iterative, consultation (outlining or from Alisa), order, harmony, phenomena and history for showing seasonal changes in plants
Tony Monk, USA	Japanese gardens embody elements of Japanese design and style, providing an environment supporting peacefulness, reflection + meditation.
Cindy Pierce, USA	Place of tranquility, + peacefulness. Simple Elegance
Ken Graff, USA	To me, what differentiates a Japanese garden from other types of gardens is beyond just the presence of native Japanese plants. There is a thoughtfulness to layout, and a sense of serenity when present

Responses on the need/significance on definition

Group Z : Con/Against/Neutral
Offshore designers with Japanese experience

Respndent	Description
Graham Hardman, UK	The answers you have sent me that you have received so far are very interesting and revealing. What they illustrate is that either people take the question at a very superficial level or, because they understand the subject, think it is impossible to create a definition and/or there is no point. I agree with this - I do not see any useful outcome from a superficial definition, which is all that is possible, given the complexity of the subject. Who would it be for? It would be like attempts to tabulate 'the Japanese garden' in the catalogues of designs during the late Edo period. They stifle creativity and use of the imagination and reduce the indefinable to a rather sad and completely inadequate formula. I would suggest you abandon the attempt. It has nothing to offer in my view. Sorry this is not what you want to hear.

Responses on the need/significance on definition

Group 6 : Con/Against/Neutral
European professionals with Japanese experience

Respndents	Description
AKA Melvyn Westreich (ISRAEL) MD - Retired Plastic Surgeon, now Gardener - Japanese garden enthusiast. Administrator - Israel Association of Japanese Gardening	I do not think there is any need for a "working" definition for Japanese. Such classification helps gardeners in planning and maintaining their gardens and visitors know what to expect before they enter the garden. The classifications of different gardens may be according to: A - Climatic or geographical regions - e.g. arid, tropical, rain forest, desert, bog, rock, etc. B - Types of plants - e.g. rose, cactus, succulents, fern, herb, vegetable etc. C - Purpose - e.g. therapeutic, children's, sensory, meditation, vegetable, community, organic, landscape, etc. D - Research, exhibition and collection - e.g. botanical, arboretum, medicinal, etc. . E - Culture - e.g. English, formal, landscape, topiary, and Japanese.
Ton Magielsen (NL) Graphic designer, japanese carpentery expert, designer, Japanese gardener and owner at Yokoso japanese gardens company.	I do not think there is a need for a definition on Japanese gardens because we already have such. Please consult the book Sakuteiki. This may be an old manual, it still stands ground. We could ask ourselves 'what is a Japanese garden', 'what are the basic ingredients', 'what is the purpose', 'what is cultural link between the garden and the people building the garden' and what is the cultural link between the garden and the spectator, Japanese or not'?

Responses on the need/significance on definition

Group 7 : Pro/For/ Neutral for Definition
European Professionals with Japanese experience

Respndent	Description
Gus Murphy 3D Japanese garden designer at www.shijima.co.uk	I think the answer to question 1 is actually a question which is 'who needs a definition and why do they need it?' I think there is a need for people to understand what they are looking for in a Japanese Garden and why they are looking for it. This can only begin to be achieved by visiting gardens and developing an understanding of the development and lineage of Japanese gardens. Once this is answered, then it is for the individual to decide in their heart on whether or not the garden meets their expectations on authenticity
Ian Fleming (UK) Head Gardener. Hadlow college of horticulture. Hadlow group. Restoring the Japanese garden at Hadlow college. Previous Head gardener of Holland Park (Kyoto garden), London.	I feel that there are certain features that already define a japanese garden. And the visitor can not help but read these in general as that they are seeing a japanese garden. I suppose This is most common of course in countries that are not Japan. Is there a need for this? I think it can not be helped...
Ton Magielsen (NL) Graphic designer, japanese carpentery expert, designer, Japanese gardener and owner at Yokoso japanese gardens company.	I do not think there is a need for a definition on Japanese gardens because we already have such. Please consult the book Sakuteiki. This may be an old manual, it still stands ground. We could ask ourselves 'what is a Japanese garden', 'what are the basic ingredients', 'what is the purpose', 'what is cultural link between the garden and the people building the garden' and what is the cultural link between the garden and the spectator, Japanese or not'?

Appendix II: Existing Description or Definition

A. Description or definition by noted scholars and designers: existing

Group 1:
Japanese Garden Professionals.

Respondent	Description
■ Hiromasa Amasaki	It is nothing but a blending of grand nature's reincarnation and creative people's work.
■ Osamu Mori	"… the special characteristics of the Japanese garden are in the ingenious artistry and symbolism which turn the miniature landscapes into something more profound and eternal."
■ Teiji Ito	"…the Japanese garden is "a recreation of idealized nature" and "a kind of spatial art in outdoor environment."
■ Seiko Goto	….lists four themes of Japanese gardens as follows: "The space to symbolize bigger nature by depicting beauty from its element….. The power of nature is a major theme…The second theme is its adaptation of features from other cultures, such as those of China and India…one of the distinguishing characteristics of the Japanese Garden is this reflection of multiple religious beliefs. The third theme is the representation of the natural scenery that appears in classical Japanese literature. The last theme is the tea ceremony….".

Group 2 :
Overseas Historian and Researcher

Respondent	Description
■ Kendall Brown	"… North American Japanese gardens are not merely translations, they are transformations calibrated to their time and place and interpreted through a social system that add complex layers of meaning."
■ Jeffery Burton	"Manzanar's Japanese gardens certainly meet these definitions of a Japanese garden, in that they depict nature in miniature….They are not recreation of surrounding environment as delivered in the Saku Tei Ki, but recollection of images of their homeland and familiar gardens. " copy of nature. It used water, stone, plant, soil to create a symbolic landscape.

■ Johann Kraftner	"… if European garden is a reflection of paradise expression ….. then the garden of the Far East in China and Japan is a reflection of nature of the country's own landscapes…. 'Spiritual' is the term often applied to describe the real meaning of Japanese gardens….".
■ John Collean and Eileen McCracken	" The Japanese garden is a unit incorporating all these components (pavilions, bridges, certain trees and plants, stone lanterns and wells) as symbols and the arrangement of the garden in a framework of water, stones and plants following certain oriental principles"

Group 3 :
Dictionary

Respondent	Description
■ Ogawa	A garden born from the work of Japanese people and continuing cotton = Japanese garden
■ Hinpei Okada	The essence of Japanese people. A copy of nature. It used water, stone, plant, soil to create a symbolic landscape.
■ Hirokazu Okusa	What is Japanese garden. A garden in which stones (including arrangement etc.) are strangely expressed
■ Izawa	I think that it is important to correct things necessary for making a Japanese garden from the daily living attitude. I feel like I'm going to meet for a while so that I can feel like I can not leave enough margin to put in my feelings after work.
■ Wikipedia.com	" Japanese gardens are traditional gardens that create miniature idealized landscapes, often in a highly abstract and stylized way."
■ Existing definition in Dictionaries	(1) "Iwanami Buddhism Dictionary" Kenkichi Ono: It is an outdoor space created for festival, ritual, entertainment, strolling, welcoming and other purposes under a set of special and seasonal aesthetic sense. Chiefly constructed with earth, stone, plants and water and generally associated with or incorporated with building. (2) "Britannica Encyclopedia": It is garden created

	directing toward formal (rock garden) and informal/natural garden based on unique set of attitudes toward nature and religion. (3) "Digital DaiJiSen": It is a general term for gardens created with unique Japanese technique. It is made mainly with natural materials and created to express nature in miniature and in symbolic form. (4) "Dai Ji Sen Dictionary": It is a Japanese style garden arranged picturesquely with pond, spring, plants, bridge, teahouse and other elements.

From Group 4 :
Japanese gardeners in Vancouver

Respondent	Description
■ Imashimizu	A space expressed in the enclosure of Japanese spirituality, aesthetic appearance, nature view
■ Ashizawa	The definition is too difficult. Is not it okay to name features, dare to define "A garden that expresses preferable landscapes among Japanese nature in water, stone, planting, landscape"
■ Kengo Sakai	A garden born from Japanese history, culture and culture. It draws out the charm of land and natural materials with a Japanese aesthetic sense and is shaped.
■ Ryo Sugiyama	It is a garden that imitated nature based on the view of the nature of the Japanese People. I am trying place stone and to prune prime according to , Japan's peculiar technology
■ Kaneda	I think that the garden is a space for man's living and for nature. So Japanese garden has Japanese identity as Japanese land, Japanese. Japanese.Is not it in the pretty garden called? The living of Japanese people and the activities of nature

■ Wakino	I think that there is a necessity to pursue inquiries such as what is Japanese garden every day. Even if it is defined, I think that it will be necessary to review it every few years. Definitely, it is obvious that something that goes out a little from there comes out. Is it a Japanese garden? It also becomes a story.

Group 4 :
Japanese gardeners in Vancouver (After discussing need for definition, they concluded to proceed with writing definition on their own words)

Respondent	Description
■ Ogawa	A garden born from the work of Japanese people and continuing cotton = Japanese garden
■ Hinpei Okada	The essence of Japanese people. A copy of nature. It used water, stone, plant, soil to create a symbolic landscape.
■ Hirokazu Okusa	What is Japanese garden. A garden in which stones (including arrangement etc.) are strangely expressed
■ Izawa	I think that it is important to correct things necessary for making a Japanese garden from the daily living attitude. I feel like I'm going to meet for a while so that I can feel like I can not leave enough margin to put in my feelings after work.
■ Kaneda	I think that the garden is a space for man's living and for nature. So Japanese garden has Japanese identity as Japanese land, Japanese. Japanese.Is not it in the pretty garden called? The living of Japanese people and the activities of nature
■ Wakino	I think that there is a necessity to pursue inquiries such as what is Japanese garden every day. Even if it is defined, I think that it will be necessary to review it every few years. Definitely, it is obvious that something that goes out a

	little from there comes out. Is it a Japanese garden? It also becomes a story.

From Group 5 :
American non professional Japanese gardeners

Respondent	Description
Patii Bower, USA	Very groomed - precise. Beauty, serenity, peace, reflection, and tailored
Connie Croy, USA	Options, geometric, iterative, consultation (outlining or from Alisa), order, harmony, phenomena and history for showing seasonal changes in plants
Tony Monk, USA	Japanese gardens embody elements of Japanese design and style, providing an environment supporting peacefulness, reflection + meditation。
Cindy Pierce, USA	Place of tranquility, + peacefulness. Simple Elegance。
Ken Graff, USA	To me, what differentiates a Japanese garden from other types of gardens is beyond just the presence of native Japanese plants. There is a thoughtfulness to layout, and a sense of serenity when present

From Group 6 :
Japanese non professionals residing abroad

Respondent (All from USA)	Description
Hiromi Komatsu	A garden that expresses nature to limited space and conditions, gets mercy and comfort The idea and view on the Japanese garden changed today. Especially the black picture.
Tsutomu Sasaki	Wabi expressing wabi, rust (immediate Japanese spirit)
Mariko Maita	Compared with the UK etc, the Japanese garden receives objectively a garden where viewers of view, spiritual and Zen-like things receive.
Hideaki Kawachi	In simple and rustic style as it is said to be Karesansui. A garden that gives peace and imagination to a person's heart. A garden that recreates nature that seems to be the original landscape of Japan from stones, water and plants.

Junko Akagi	The Japanese garden is more like an art ART rather than a living style in the shape of a pure garden.

Group 7
Japanese Landscape Professionals

■Ryuichi Wakisaka wakisaka-r82ac@mlit.go.jp	The Japanese garden is a garden style backed by Japanese culture and history, reflecting ideas of each period background. Also used as a place of Japanese culture such as tea ceremony. Is it such a form? There are difficulties like defining Japanese food.
■Masao Ootsuka ootsuka@jcom.home.ne.jpMasao	Looking at the figure of nature around us, capturing, condensing what I felt from it, expressed using natural materials
■Akira Miyake miyake.bon81@jcom.home.ne.jp	· A garden that expresses natural beauty · Expression of Japanese aesthetic sense (Wabi, Sabi, Ikebana) using planting, water, stone, sand etc · Expression of relaxation of the four seasons
■Kazuhiko Fujinami fujinami@tlp.co.jp	A garden in which nature and artifacts made in accordance with Japanese aesthetic sense are harmonized
■Naofumi Ochiai ochiai@bunkanken.tokyo	The Japanese garden is a ruler that predicts the change of nature by a custom made by reflecting spirituality to nature
■ShinAkasak AKASAKA.shin@rk.sfc.co.jp	Since ancient times, we live in a country with this beautiful four seasons We are the crystal of our efforts to create a wish for the Japanese to respect and respect the nature and put peace of mind that comes from there close to ourselves.
■Takashi Kikutani kikuya@k-ohba.co.jp	Expressing the natural environment of nature, the origins of nature, the four seasons, traditions, culture, etc. in a limited area by natural materials (stone, water, earth, wood (plants)
■Shigetani Edayoshi Email edayoshi@galc.co.jp	A garden is a place to express the feelings of the owner. A space that is longing for the landscape, expressing peace
■ kihiko Torikoshi torigoe@urbangreen.or.jp	◯ Space that communicates symbiosis with nature not only to the form but also to the heart ◯ Space that can be integrated continuously with the natural landscape and continuously in the area ◯ In any case, what you can enjoy enjoying people and being able to relax is prerequisite ◯ For

	that, you need a way to show and a story
■Masayoshi Taga pepsi111@mist.ocn.ne.jp	It reflects the change of the season, makes you feel at ease, tranquility, mystique, depending on the season, it also makes you feel glamorous and Voiddness. It is a garden with unparalleled sensibility in the world.
■Noriaki Tanaka tanaka-nori@ej-hds.co.jp	Regardless of its size and scale, it refers to the garden created by the Japanese aesthetic sense that eliminated the awe and waste of the forest and nature that was the basis of Japanese spirituality. Moreover, it is a space that does not get tired of creatures and winds gathered in the quiet space. (Show diverse appearance)
■Haruto Kobayashi haruto@tle.co.jp jushimatu@aol.com	What I think is necessary when discussing the definition (1) To clarify to some extent the origins and origin of something about what is the Japanese garden (2) Although it was a story from an emotional perspective, is there a logical (scientific) deployment ...? (3) spiritual foundation of Japanese, spiritual DNA from the Jomon period (4) Spirituality to study Shinto and Buddhism (5) Nature worship, the lawn philosophy <--- (6) spiritual DNA ? · The Japanese garden is an art that photographed the whole phenomenon photographically. · There are naturalistic and humanistic methods as representation methods.
■ Jyun Ishikawa	It is a proud expression in the world that makes me feel at ease by composing people's sensibility and skill to convey the archipelago nature
■ Kazuo Mitsuhashi ingo@mitsuhashi-teien.com	The origin of the Japanese garden is in the stone shape which begins with the stone pavement, the stone boundary, but it made it into the space holding the comfort and healing of the spirit by adding natural materials to it. Depending on the position to make and the position to appreciate, its values will differ. Especially Japanese garden thinks its background includes diverse cultural elements.
■Konatsu Himeda himeda@onyx.ocn.ne.jp	It is difficult to define, but nervousness and artificial balance brings tension beauty and I can capture

1-A. Description or definition

> *Developing definition*

Group 1 :
Japanese Garden Professionals.

Respondent	Description
■ Makoto Suzuki	"Even though Takenosuke Tatsui, stated in 1991 , "that there is no firm definition of Japanese garden which strikes to the essence of Japanese garden, it is important to develop proper terminology and definition for Japanese garden, if one considers it as a subject of academic/scientific work." He does not offer a definition of Japanese (traditional) garden.
■ Yukio Yashiro	"Japanese Garden is truly in natural style while a western garden presents very formal man made organization as illustrated in Italian and French Garden. Contrasting to English Scenery (natural) Garden which presents a part of nature, the Japanese Garden is not just a copy of the nature but symbolization of the nature by use of plants, rocks, earth mound and water."
■ Makoto Nakamura	"Japanese garden is symbolic miniature garden in contrast to realistic scenery garden of England."

1-B. Description or definition by Japanese professionals in Canada: proposed

> *Developing definition*

From Group 4 :
Japanese gardeners in Vancouver

Respondent	Description
■ Imashimizu	A space expressed in the enclosure of Japanese spirituality, aesthetic appearance, nature view
■ Ashizawa	The definition is too difficult. Is not it okay to name features, dare to define "A garden that expresses preferable landscapes among Japanese nature in water, stone, planting, landscape"
■ Kengo Sakai	A garden born from Japanese history, culture and culture. It draws out the charm of land and natural materials with a Japanese aesthetic sense and is shaped.
■ Ryo Sugiyama	It is a garden that imitated nature based on the view of the nature of the Japanese People. I am trying place stone and to prune prime according to , Japan's peculiar technology

> *Developing definition*

Group 4 :

Japanese gardeners in Vancouver (After discussing need for definition, they concluded to proceed with writing definition on their own words)

Respondent	Description
■ Ogawa	A garden born from the work of Japanese people and continuing cotton = Japanese garden
■ Hinpei Okada	The essence of Japanese people. A copy of nature. It used water, stone, plant, soil to create a symbolic landscape.
■ Hirokazu Okusa	What is Japanese garden. A garden in which stones (including arrangement etc.) are strangely expressed
■ Izawa	I think that it is important to correct things necessary for making a Japanese garden from the daily living attitude. I feel like I'm going to meet for a while so that I can feel like I can not leave enough margin to put in my feelings after work.

1-C. Description or definition by non professionals in USA: proposed

> *Developing definition*

From Group 5 :

American non professional Japanese gardeners

Respondent	Description
Patii Bower, USA	Very groomed - precise. Beauty, serenity, peace, reflection, and tailored
Connie Croy, USA	Options, geometric, iterative, consultation (outlining or from Alisa), order, harmony, phenomena and history for showing seasonal changes in plants
Tony Monk, USA	Japanese gardens embody elements of Japanese design and style, providing an environment supporting peacefulness, reflection + meditation。
Cindy Pierce, USA	Place of tranquility, + peacefulness. Simple Elegance。

| Ken Graff, USA | To me, what differentiates a Japanese garden from other types of gardens is beyond just the presence of native Japanese plants. There is a thoughtfulness to layout, and a sense of serenity when present |

Developing definition

From Group 6 :
Japanese non professionals residing abroad

Respondent (All from USA)	Description
Hiromi Komatsu	A garden that expresses nature to limited space and conditions, gets mercy and comfort The idea and view on the Japanese garden changed today. Especially the black picture.
Tsutomu Sasaki	Wabi expressing wabi, rust (immediate Japanese spirit)
Mariko Maita	Compared with the UK etc, the Japanese garden receives objectively a garden where viewers of view, spiritual and Zen-like things receive.
Hideaki Kawachi	In simple and rustic style as it is said to be Karesansui. A garden that gives peace and imagination to a person's heart. A garden that recreates nature that seems to be the original landscape of Japan from stones, water and plants.

Junko Akagi	The Japanese garden is more like an art ART rather than a living style in the shape of a pure garden.

Developing definition

Group 7
Japanese Landscape Professionals

Respondent (All from USA)	Description
■ Jyun Ishikawa	It is a proud expression in the world that makes me feel at ease by composing people's sensibility and skill to convey the archipelago nature
■ Kazuo Mitsuhashi ingo@mitsuhashi-teien.com	The origin of the Japanese garden is in the stone shape which begins with the stone pavement, the stone boundary, but it made it into the space holding the comfort and healing of the spirit by adding natural materials to it. Depending on the position to make and the position to appreciate, its values will differ. Especially Japanese garden thinks its background includes diverse cultural elements.
■Konatsu Himeda himeda@onyx.ocn.ne.jp	It is difficult to define, but nervousness and artificial balance brings tension beauty and I can capture
■Matsukawa	There is nothing you can not explain when creating a garden.
■ Takahiro Naka	In the field of art, it is difficult to include modernity. We can update them.

Appendix II : Evaluation of Existing Description or Definition

1. Evaluation of definition by Japanese professionals

Evaluating definition

Group 1:
Japanese Garden Professionals.

Respondent	Description	Attribute	
■ Hiromasa Amasaki	It is nothing but a blending of grand nature's reincarnation and creative people's work.	1 5	
■ Osamu Mori	"… the special characteristics of the Japanese garden are in the ingenious artistry and symbolism which turn the miniature landscapes into something more profound and eternal."	1 5	
■ Teiji Ito	"…the Japanese garden is "a recreation of idealized nature" and "a kind of spatial art in outdoor environment."	1 5	
■ Seiko Goto	…lists four themes of Japanese gardens as follows: "The space to symbolize bigger nature by depicting beauty from its element…… The power of nature is a major theme…The second theme is its adaptation of features from other cultures, such as those of China and India…one of the distinguishing characteristics of the Japanese Garden is this reflection of multiple religious beliefs. The third theme is the representation of the natural scenery that appears in classical Japanese literature. The last theme is the tea ceremony….".	1 2 3 5	

Evaluating definition

Group 2:
Overseas Historian and Researcher

Respondent	Description	Attribute	
■ Kendall Brown	"… North American Japanese gardens are not merely translations, they are transformations calibrated to their time and place and interpreted through a social system that add complex layers of meaning."	1 2	
■ Jeffery Burton	"Manzanar's Japanese gardens certainly meet these definitions of a Japanese garden, in that they depict nature in miniature….They are not recreation of surrounding environment as delivered in the Saku Tei Ki, but recollection of images of their homeland and familiar gardens. " copy of nature. It used water, stone, plant, soil to create a symbolic landscape.	1 2 3 4 5	
■ Johann Kraftner	"… if European garden is a reflection of paradise expression ….. then the garden of the Far East in China and Japan is a reflection of nature of the country's own landscapes…. 'Spiritual' is the term often applied to describe the real meaning of Japanese gardens….".	1 5	
■ John Collean and Eileen McCracken	" The Japanese garden is a unit incorporating all these components (pavilions, bridges, certain trees and plants, stone lanterns and wells) as symbols and the arrangement of the garden in a framework of water, stones and plants following certain oriental principles"	1 2 3 4	

Evaluating definition	提案の定義の　評価

From Group 4 :

Japanese gardeners in Vancouver

Respondent	Description	Attribute	
■今清水 Imashimizu	日本人の精神性、美観、自然観を囲いの中に表した空間 A space expressed in the enclosure of Japanese spirituality, aesthetic appearance, nature view	1 5	
■芦沢 Ashizawa	定義付は難しすぎる。特徴を挙げるので良いのではないか、あえて定義付を「日本の自然の中好ましい景観を水、石、植栽、景観に表現する庭」 The definition is too difficult. Is not it okay to name features, dare to define "A garden that expresses preferable landscapes among Japanese nature in water,stone, planting, landscape	2	
■酒井兼五 Kengo Sakai	日本の歴史、風土、文化から生まれた庭園 土地や自然素材の魅力を、日本人的美的感覚をもって引き出し、形にされる。 A garden born from Japanese history, culture and culture. It draws out the charmof land and natural materials with a Japanese aesthetic sense and is shaped.	1	
■杉山龍 Ryo Sugiyama	日本人の自然観に基づき自然に倣った庭園であり、日本独特の技術・石の据え やすかしの剪定をしようしている。新渡戸稲造記念庭園 It is a garden that imitated nature based on the view of the nature of the Japanese People. I am trying place stone and to prune prime according to , Japan's peculiar technology	1 3 5	

2. Evaluation of definition by Japanese professionals in Canada

Evaluating definition	提案の定義の　評価

Group 4 :

Japanese gardeners in Vancouver (After discussing need for definition, they concluded to proceed with writing definition on their own words)

Respondent	Description	Attribute	
■小川 Ogawa	日本人の営みから生まれ連綿と続いている庭＝日本庭園 A garden born from the work of Japanese people and continuing cotton = Japanese garden	1	
■岡田伸平 Hinpei Okada	日本人の持つ本質。自然の写し。水、石、植物、土を使って象徴的な風景を創り出したもの。 The essence of Japanese people. A copy of nature. It used water, stone, plant, soil to create a symbolic landscape.	1 3 4	
■大草広和 Hirokazu Okusa	日本庭園とは。石組み（配置等を含めて）の妙が表現されている庭 What is Japanese garden. A garden in which stones (including arrangement etc.) are strangely expressed	4	
■井沢 Izawa	日本庭園を作るにあたり必要な事は日々の生活姿勢から正していく事が大事であると思います。一期一会という気持ちで施主と向い合い余力を残せない状態に作業後あるくらいに気持ちを入れ込む。 I think that it is important to correct things necessary for making a Japanese garden from the daily living attitude. I feel like I'm going to meet for a while so that I can feel like I can not leave enough margin to put in my feelings after work.	5	

Evaluating definition　　　　　　　　提案の定義の　評価

From Group 4
Japanese gardeners in Vancouver

Respondent	Description	Attribute	
■金田 Kaneda	庭とは人間の暮らしと自然への営み空間だと思います。 では日本庭園とは日本国土、日本語、日本人としてのアイデンティティを持つという事前ていての庭ではないでしょうか。 日本人の暮らしと自然との営み空間 I think that the garden is a space for man's living and for nature. So Japanese garden has Japanese identity as Japanese land, Japanese. Japanese.Is not it in the pretty garden called? The living of Japanese people and the activities of nature	5	
■脇野 Wakino	日本庭園とは、なんぞやという探求は日常にしていく必要性はあると思います。 たとえ定義付けしたとしても、数年毎に見直す必要は出てくると思います。 定義付ければ、そこから少しはずれるものが出てくるのは明白。 それは日本庭園なのか？という話にもなってくる。 I think that there is a necessity to pursue inquiries such as what is Japanese garden every day. Even if it is defined, I think that it will be necessary to review it every few years. Definitely, it is obvious that something that goes out a little from there comes out. Is it a Japanese garden? It also becomes a story.	2	

3. Evaluation of definition by Japanese professionals in Japan

Evaluating definition　　　　　　　　提案の定義の　評価

Group 7
Japanese Landscape Professionals

Respondent	Description	Attribute	
■Ryuichi Wakisaka 脇坂隆一 wakisaka-r82ac@mlit.go.jp	日本庭園とは、日本の風土、歴史に裏打ちされた庭園様式であり、各時代背景の思想が反映されている。また茶道などの日本文化の場として活用される。 といった形でしょうか？和食を定義するような難しさがあります。 The Japanese garden is a garden style backed by Japanese culture and history, reflecting ideas of each period background. Also used as a place of Japanese culture such as tea ceremony. Is it such a form? There are difficulties like defining Japanese food.	1.5	
■Masao Ootsuka 大塚政雄 ootsuka@jcom.home.ne.jpMasao	身のまわりの自然の姿を見つめ、とらえ、そこから感じ得たものを凝縮し、自然の素材を用い表現したもの Looking at the figure of nature around us, capturing, condensing what I felt from it, expressed using natural materials	1.5	
■Akira Miyake 三宅章 miyake.bon81@jcom.home.ne.jp	・自然の美を表現する庭　・素材として植栽、水、石、砂などを用いて日本人の美意識（わび、さび、もののあわれ）を表現　・四季のうつろいを表現 · A garden that expresses natural beauty · Expression of Japanese aesthetic sense (Wabi, Sabi, Ikebana) using planting, water, stone, sand etc · Expression of relaxation of the four seasons	1.3.4.	
■Kazuhiko Fujinami 藤浪和彦 fujinami@tlp.co.jp 高野ランドスケーププランニング	日本の美的感覚にもとづいて造られた自然と人工物が調和した庭 A garden in which nature and artifacts made in accordance with Japanese aesthetic sense are harmonized	1.2.3	

Evaluating definition 提案の定義の 評価

Group 7
Japanese Landscape Professionals

Respondent (All from USA)	Description	Attribute	
■Naofumi Ochiai 落合直文 ochiai@bunkanken.tokyo 文化環境設計研究所	日本庭園とは、自然に対する精神性を映し込んだ仕つらえによる自然の変化を予測する物差し The Japanese garden is a ruler that predicts the change of nature by a custom made by reflecting spirituality to nature	5	
■Shin Akasak 赤坂真 住友林業株式会社 AKASAKA.shin@rk.sfc.co.jp	古来より、この美しい四季を持つ国で暮らす我々日本人が自然に対する尊敬の念とそこから得られる心の安らぎを自らの近くに置くことを願い創造しようとした努力の結晶です。 Since ancient times, we live in a country with this beautiful four seasons We are the crystal of our efforts to create a wish for the Japanese to respect and respect the nature and put peace of mind that comes from there close to ourselves.	5	
■Takashi Kikutani 菊谷隆 (株)オオバ kikuya@k-ohba.co.jp	自然素材(石、水、土、木(植物))等により、日本の自然環境、自然の成り立ち、四季、伝統、文化等を限られたエリアの中で表現したもの Expressing the natural environment of nature, the origins of nature, the four seasons, traditions, culture, etc. in a limited area by natural materials (stone, water, earth, wood (plants)	1.3.4.	
■Shigetani Edayoshi 枝吉茂種 (株)グラック Email edayoshi@galc.co.jp	庭園とは所有者の思いを表現する場。景観へのあこがれであり、やすらぎを表わす空間。 A garden is a place to express the feelings of the owner. A space that is longing for the landscape, expressing peace	5	

Evaluating definition 提案の定義の 評価

Group 7
Japanese Landscape Professionals

Respondent (All from USA)	Description	Attribute	
■ kihiko Torikoshi 鳥越照彦 torigoe@urbangreen.or.jp	○自然との共生を形だけでなく、心に伝える空間 ○自然の景観と融合し、地域において持続的に継承可能な空間 ○いずれにせよ、人が来て楽しめること、リラックスできることが前提条件 ○そのためには、見せ方やストーリーが必要 ○ Space that communicates symbiosis with nature not only to the form but also to he heart ○ Space that can be integrated continuously with the natural landscape and continuously in the area ○ In any case, what you can enjoy enjoying people and being able to relax is prerequisite ○ For that, you need a way to show and a story	1.5	
■Masayoshi Taga 多賀正義 pepsi111@mist.ocn.ne.jp	季節の変化を写し出し、安らぎ、静けさ、神秘性を感じさせ季節によっては、華やかさ、Voiddnessも感じさせる。世界にも類を見ない感性を持った庭園である。 It reflects the change of the season, makes you feel at ease, tranquility, mystique, depending on the season, it also makes you feel glamorous and Voiddness. It is a garden with unparalleled sensibility in the world.	5	
■Noriaki Tanaka 田中紀昭 tanaka-nori@ej-hds.co.jp	その大きさや規模にかかわらず日本人の精神性の基となった森や自然に対する畏敬の念や無駄を排除した日本人の美意識により作られた庭を言う。又、その静かな空間に集う生きものや風やいつでも飽きない空間である。(多様な姿を見せる) Regardless of its size and scale, it refers to the garden created by the Japanese aesthetic sense that eliminated the awe and waste of the forest and nature that was the basis of Japanese spirituality. Moreover, it is a space that does not get tired of creatures and winds gathered in the quiet space. (Show diverse appearance)	5	

Evaluating definition 提案の定義の 評価

Group 7
Japanese Landscape Professionals

Respondent (All from USA)	Description	Attribute	
■Haruto Kobayashi 小林治人 haruto@tle.co.jp jushimatu@aol.com	定義を論ずる時必要と思うこと (1) そもそも日本庭園とは何かについてその<u>起源、源流</u>をある程度明確にすること (2) 情緒的視座からのお話でしたが論理的(科学的)な展開が…？ (3) 日本人の精神的基盤、縄文時代からの精神的DNA (4) 神仏習合する精神性 (5) 自然崇拝、芝生の哲学<---(6) 精神的DNA ・日本庭園は森羅万象を写意的に編纂した芸術である。 ・表現手法としては自然主義的、人間主義的な手法がある。 What I think is necessary when discussing the definition (1) To clarify to some extent the origins and origin of something about what is the Japanese garden (2) Although it was a story from an emotional perspective, is there a logical (scientific) deployment ...? (3) spiritual foundation of Japanese, spiritual DNA from the Jomon period (4) Spirituality to study Shinto and Buddhism (5) Nature worship, the lawn philosophy <--- (6) spiritual DNA ? · The Japanese garden is an art that photographed the whole phenomenon photographically. · There are naturalistic and humanistic methods as representation methods.	1.2.5	

Evaluating definition 提案の定義の 評価

Group 7
Japanese Landscape Professionals

Respondent (All from USA)	Description	Attribute	
■ Jyun Ishikawa 石川純	列島の自然をうつすことを人の感性と技術で構成した心やすらぐ世界に誇る表現です It is a proud expression in the world that makes me feel at ease by composing people's sensibility and skill to convey the archipelago nature	5	
■ Kazuo Mitsuhashi 三橋一夫 ingo@mitsuhashi-teien.com 日本庭園協会	日本庭園の源流は石盤、石境に始まる石の造形にあるが、自然の木をそれに加味して精神の安らぎと癒しを内に抱いた空間に作りげたものである。作る立場と鑑賞する立場によって、その価値観異なってくる。特に日本庭園はその背景には多様な文化的要素が含まれている、と考える。The origin of the Japanese garden is in the stone shape which begins with the stone pavement, the stone boundary, but it made it into the space holding the comfort and healing of the spirit by adding natural materials to it. Depending on the position to make and the position to appreciate, its values will differ. Especially Japanese garden thinks its background includes diverse cultural elements.	1.2.3.4.5	
■Konatsu Himeda 姫田小夏 アジア・ビズ・フォーラム himeda@onyx.ocn.ne.jp	定義するのは難しいですが、自然と人工のバランスがもたらす緊張美と私はとらえますIt is difficult to define, but nervousness and artificial balance brings tension beauty and I can capture	1.	
■Matsukawa 松川	庭をつくる時に説明できない事は無い方が良い。 There is nothing you can not explain when creating a garden.		
■仲隆裕 Takahiro Naka	芸術の分野では、現代性を含めると難しい。自分達が更新して行けば良い.In the field of art, it is difficult to include modernity. We can update them.		

Appendix III : Responses from the Initial Workshop on Image of Japanese Garden

■鳥居ヒューゴ
三渓園（横浜）　大切な人に見せたい庭
地元の日本庭園であり、幼いころから心に近い庭である。
庭の裏の断崖絶壁と海は横浜の大事な景色である。

OKAZAKI VILLA GARDEN
2年間精魂込めて作った庭である。
オーナーが嬉しそうに何回も庭を回られた時の感動は忘れられない。

■植彌加藤造園株式会社　川村茂好
庭園名　北村美術館　四君子苑
・石像美術品の宝庫といわれるのにふさわしく庭園内には重文2点を含む多数の名石像物があり、美術館のように楽しませてくれる。時に鎌倉時代の宝塔基礎石を見立物の手水鉢としたものは、側面四面全てに近江模様の対向孔雀を立体感ある半肉彫にした豪華なもので、圧倒されました。
・敷地面積は狭いものの、横を鴨川が流れ、大文字山をはじめとする東山を望む、ロケーションはすばらしい。
・施主北村謹次郎の思いを佐野越守が表現した独特のこだわりが庭に詰め込まれたという感じで、盛りだくさんの見せ場がある。その中で、表門から玄関につづく奈良の金棒石で敷き詰められた延段は、目地の合わせ具合と表面の慣れ具合が美しかったです。
・作庭当初から、庭を管理されている方があり、時代は変わってもみる受け継がれる思いが繋がっている雰囲気が伝わってきました。

■林寛也
何有荘庭園
瀧の高さに驚かされた庭です。四季の様々な顔も好きで、何より、自分が一番長く携わっている庭というのが私の理由です

■中村（６６歳）
土木工事に40年従事し庭についてはまったくの素人です。

龍安寺　哲学的になれると言うか？庭を見て自分自身も見直し、無念無想、心境により変化する庭と感じる。
何有荘　瑞瀧の瀧　今では見る事ができないが洋館2Fの窓からみる滝もよかった。
御所　一般公開の時　休日の時は散歩がてらに行く。赤松の柔らかさ、暖かさを感じる木があった。
對龍山荘　庭と感じた

■無記名
栗林公園　敷地の中に色々なストーリーを感じて面白い。
広い庭園が好きです。

■高桑
自分の好きな庭
①渉成園
池泉回遊式の庭であり印月池から見える景色が素晴らしいと思います。

②大徳寺
低木に仕立てられた多数の松が印象的で大変インパクトがありました。

③詩仙堂
石川文山の庭園で四面三十六人の中国の詩人の壁画と簡潔に収められた空間や鹿威しの静けさを破る演出がお気に入りです。

■加藤武史
對龍山荘　過去に見学に行かせていただき、感動した。私の中では最高の庭園。景のとりこみ、庭屋一如、昔の演出等あらゆる技法が集結した究極の庭園

桂離宮　樹木は実にシンプルだが、建造物、庭園施設のクオリティ。こだわりが各所で楽しめる庭園景の遮へいが見事。■
無記名
円通寺　現在でも周囲に高い建築物がなく比叡山の借景がきれいであるため

■無記名
大徳寺狐篷庵
二条城二ノ丸庭園との作意の違いと赤土の斬新さ

■無記名
桂離宮
月をテーマに
庭の構成がブレてない所

Appendix IV : Forecasting Future Trend for Japanese Garden

Introduction

Following illustrates an attempt to identify future trends for Japanese gardens (abroad) through graphically presenting, summarizing and analyzing gardens as cited by five leading designers and scholars on Japanese garden.

They include Makoto Suzuki, "19-20 th Centuries of Japanese Garden (Monograph), 2001, Christian Tagsold, "Spaces in Translation", 2017 and Kendal Brown, "Visionary Landscape", 2017.

Gardens cited are plotted on a diagram of concentric circles with two axis to compare their positional difference. These axis include: (Traditional) Evolution with Nature & Spirituality and (Modern) Art/Aesthetic: Visual on horizontal axis and Evolving & Expanding Uses: Multiple and Singular Use: Contemplation on vertical axis.

Further citations by Masuno Shomyo, "The Modern Japanese Garden", 2002, and Norihisa Okada, "Begin the Japanese Garden", 2008, "One Hundred Gardens and Designers" by Hitoshi Toyokura, 2014 and those cited by five garden masters as listed by Kendall, 2017 Brown.

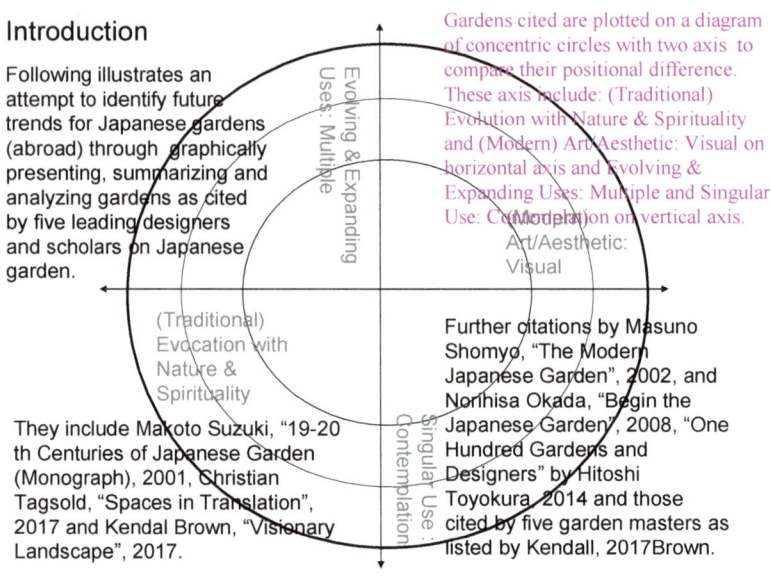

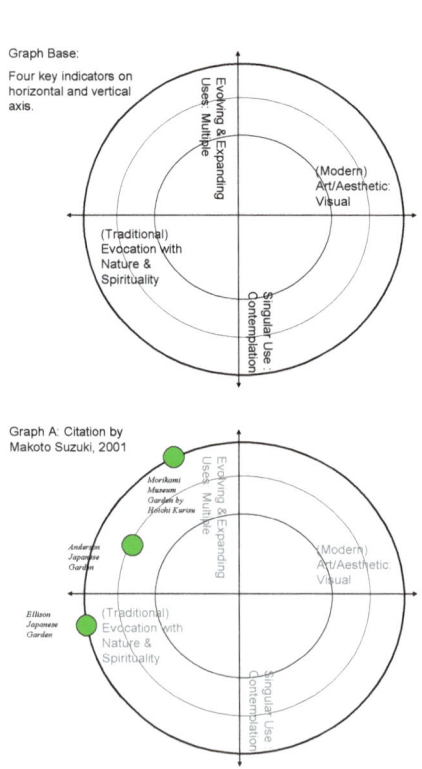

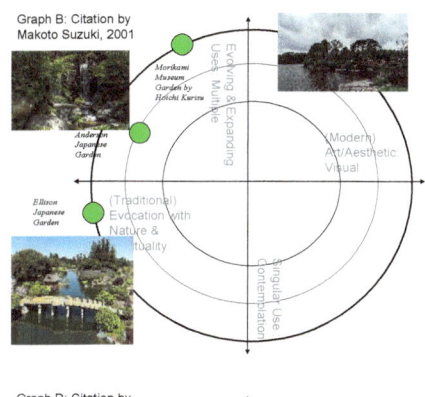

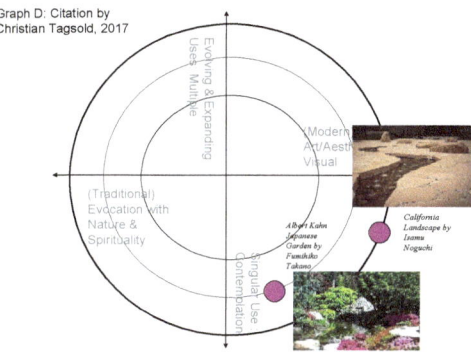

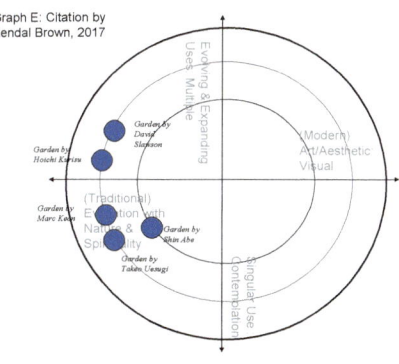

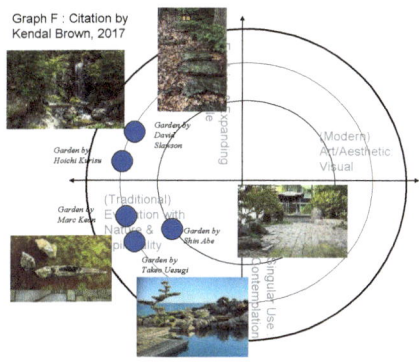

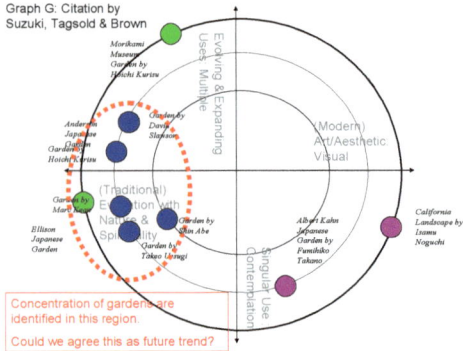

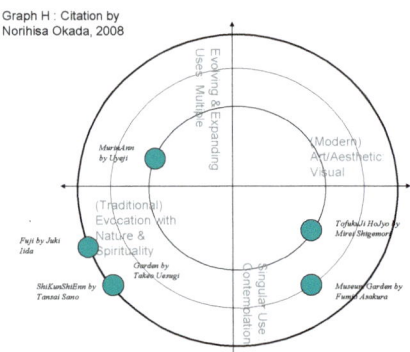

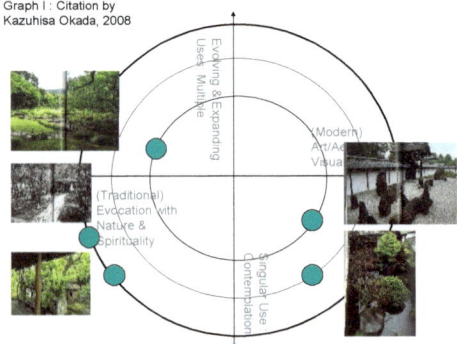

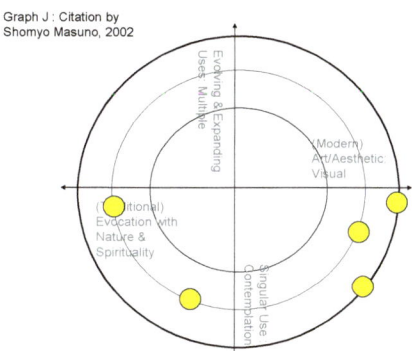

Graph J : Citation by Shomyo Masuno, 2002

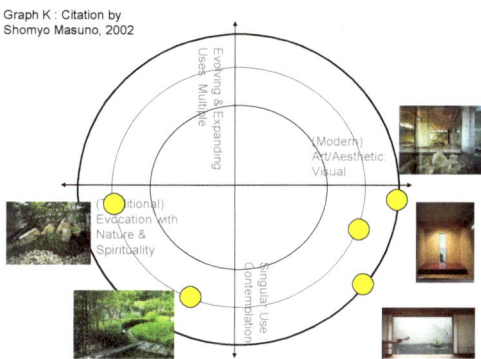

Graph K : Citation by Shomyo Masuno, 2002

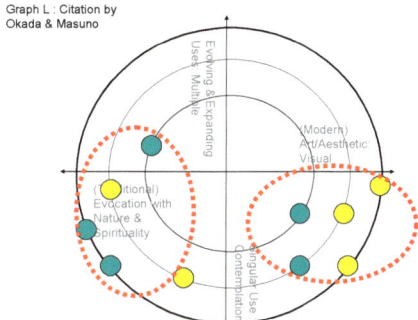

Graph L : Citation by Okada & Masuno

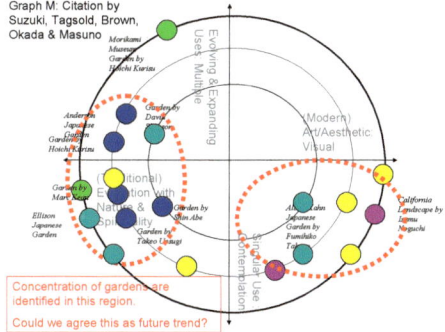

Graph M: Citation by Suzuki, Tagsold, Brown, Okada & Masuno

Concentration of gardens are identified in this region.

Could we agree this as future trend?

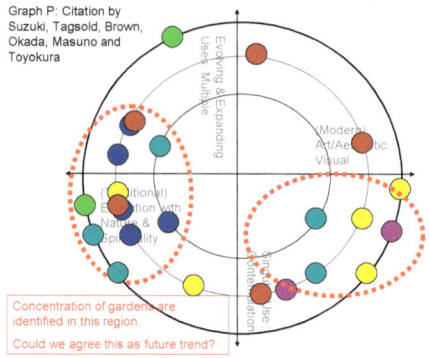

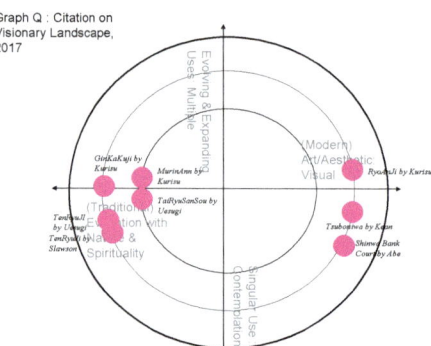

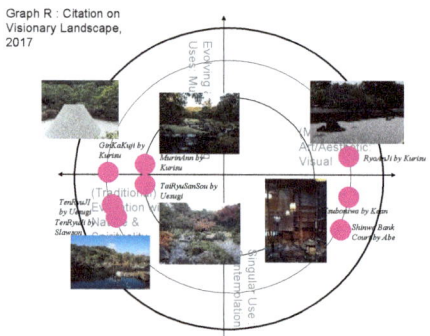

Graph S : Composite

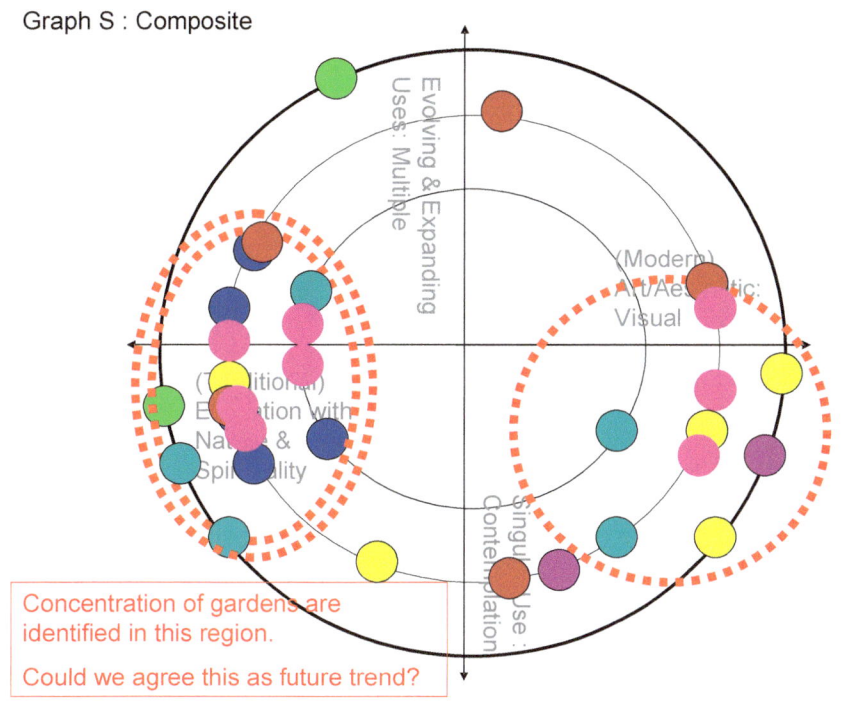

Concentration of gardens are identified in this region.

Could we agree this as future trend?

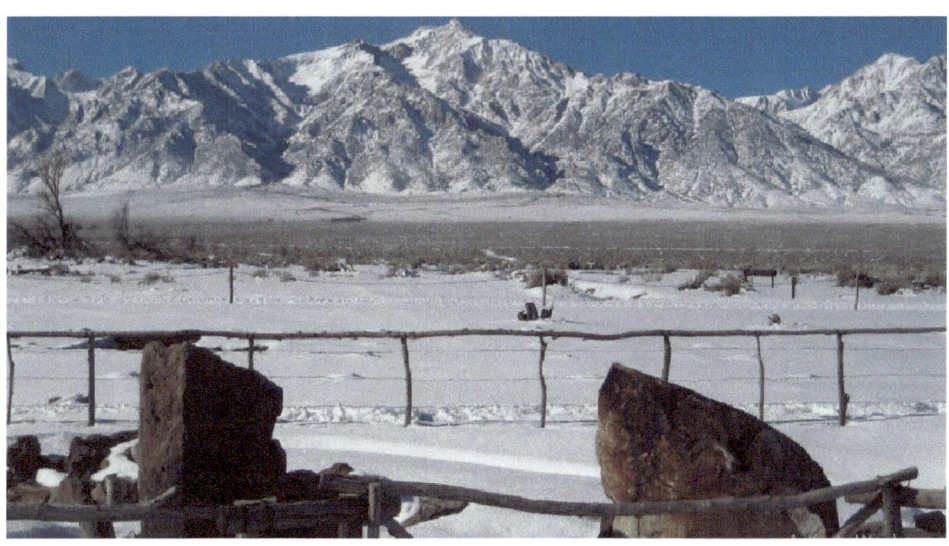

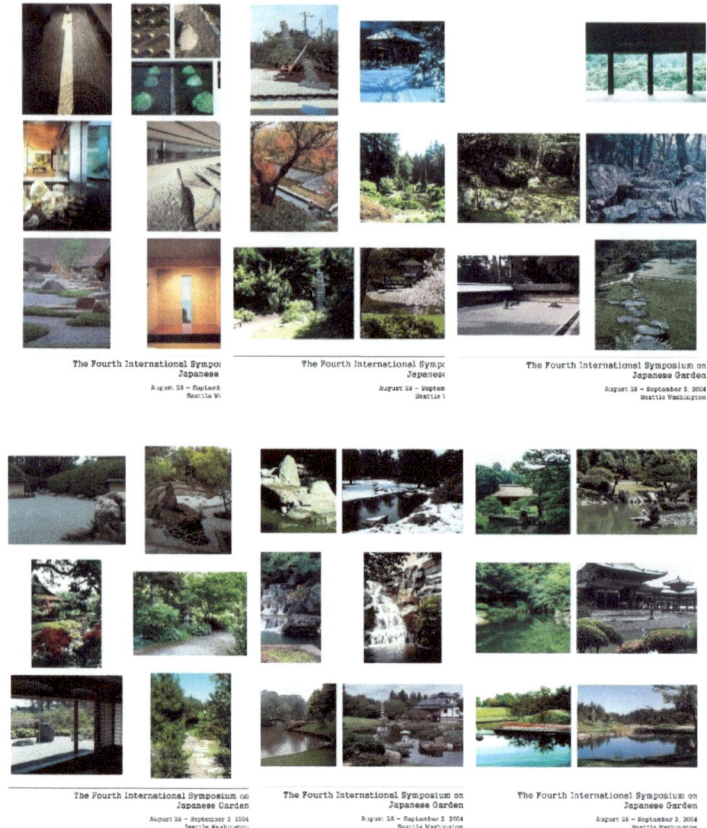

Koichi Kobayashi is a Japanese-American urban designer and landscape architect currently based in Seattle, Washington. Born in Kurayoshi, Tottori, Japan in 1945, Kobayashi has more than 50 years' experience in a diverse field of landscape architecture, including planning, design, teaching, and community development. He is a 1972 graduate of the University of California, Berkeley, and in 1968, of Kyoto University. After completing his time in teaching, public practice and managing his own office over thirty years working on projects from USA, Canada and Japan, 2001 to 2007, he worked in China and in Dubai where he worked on large-scale environmental and landscape planning projects in China, the Middle East and India. In this position, he mentored young professionals from around the world. He is currently the principal of Kobayashi Design in Seattle, and is researching and promoting the cause of Japanese gardens abroad, including supporting "Friends of Saving the Legacy of Seko Garden" 2 as a principal. In 2018 Kobayashi was designated Honorary Professor at Eimei University, San Mateo, California.

www.ingramcontent.com/pod-product-compliance
Lightning Source LLC
Chambersburg PA
CBHW040320220526
45473CB00009B/2500